BACK IN THE
DRIVING SEAT

BACK IN THE DRIVING SEAT

CREATING YOUR OWN BUSINESS RECOVERY

GEORGE MORDAUNT

MERCIER PRESS
IRISH PUBLISHER – IRISH STORY

To the people of Ireland who continue to struggle
financially. I hope and pray that this book helps.

MERCIER PRESS

Cork

www.mercierpress.ie

© George Mordaunt, 2013

George can be contacted through www.georgemordaunt.com or on
Twitter @GMordaunt

ISBN: 978 1 78117 139 4

10 9 8 7 6 5 4 3 2 1

A CIP record for this title is available from the British Library

Printed and bound in the EU.

Contents

Introduction

Faced with crisis, the man of character falls back on himself.
He imposes his own stamp of action, takes responsibility for
it, makes it his own.

Charles de Gaulle

For me it wasn't just another December morning. It was a day
tinged with excitement but also a little tiredness, as I continued
to juggle the day job, running my car sales business, and the
promotional tour of my recently published book *Shepherd's Pie*.
It was an exhilarating time and I was very proud of the book,
but now my words and actions were being scrutinised, not just
by the media, but by the many distressed people around the
country as we all tried desperately to overcome the enormous
challenges of Ireland's economic crisis. At times this scrutiny
felt like a heavy weight to a newbie like me. Then one phone
call changed my perspective.

The first thing I noticed was how soft the man's voice was.
He asked, 'Is that George Mordaunt?', and when I confirmed
that it was, went on to tell me that he had recently decided
that he couldn't go on. 'I walked to my garden shed late one
evening a few weeks ago. It was dark and cold. I stacked some
empty paint cans on top of each other and tied a rope around
the roof support. I stood on the cans in my bare feet. I paused
and considered what I was about to do and then you popped
into my mind. I thought about what I had heard you say on

the radio recently. Your comments rang true for me and so I stepped down and decided that I was going to persevere and call you to tell you that I am going to buy my next car from you. It might take me twelve years, but when I do buy, I'll buy from you.'

It had taken that man almost three weeks to call me. I spoke with him for about fifteen minutes. I urged him to come and meet me, but he wouldn't. The call ended. I never got his name and I don't know what happened to him. I can only hope that someday he will discover that he had as much of an effect on me as I apparently had on him. His phone call was a tipping point for me. My decision to tell the story of my financial collapse had opened the door to that dark room in which many others also found themselves, but now I realised I needed to do more.

After *Shepherd's Pie* was published, the overwhelming response I received from Irish people from all walks of life demonstrated to me that people wanted to know how to resolve their difficulties with their banks, their properties and their business on a practical level. Between October and December 2011 I met hundreds of business owners, and the two questions that I was consistently asked were:

(a) How did you get the banks off your back? and
(b) Can you elaborate on exactly the steps that you took towards business and financial recovery?

That was it. A practical, tangible solution is what those people wanted.

Shepherd's Pie had described my emotional correction – the realisation and acceptance of where I was, the intensity of the problem and the trigger to fight back. *Back in the Driving Seat* is a step-by-step guide to what I did to ensure the survival and ongoing rehabilitation of my business, how I am dealing with a property portfolio in negative equity and, ultimately, how to tackle the elephant in the room: hard-core debt.

I wrote this story as it unfolded, and it is my hope that by the time the reader has reached the last few chapters of the book the entire process has become very clear. My recovery was not a strategy, but an acceptance that I could only take one day at a time and deal with the issues of that day. This story unfolds in the same manner. At the end of each chapter I have included a key lesson to help summarise what I have learned over the period of my recovery.

Recovery and all that it entails is within your grasp – now you must make it your own. You must decide to become an active participant in your own rescue.

That process starts here.

1

Seat belts on,
no turning back now

Feelings or emotions are the universal language and are to be
honoured. They are the authentic expression of who you are
at your deepest place.

Judith Wright

For many people affected by the global economic collapse there
is a common denominator – the point where they lost control.
Control is critical in many aspects of life. Despite my best efforts
to tell my story as honestly as I could, I found myself having
mixed emotions as I put the finishing touches to *Shepherd's Pie*
in the summer of 2011. On one hand I felt positive and upbeat
about the final chapter of the story – thrilled to have found
the words to express how I felt with that last sentence. I had
been troubled by where the story would lead because I really
didn't know the ending when I started writing and, truthfully,
I still had no idea where it would take me. I was about to go
public with my story of recovery, how I had taken control of
my financial life and made the banks disappear from my life,
knowing full well that at any point it could all blow up in my
face. I needed to stop and consider what was around the corner.

While I was writing *Shepherd's Pie* I hoped that the story would be warmly received, but sitting at a laptop at 2.30 a.m., reading what I had just written, I frequently wondered if I was about to mortify myself and my family by making public such a private story – a story that was epic in our family life, but which I doubted anyone else would give a shit about or be able to relate to. But I was committed, there was no turning back, it was time to have the courage of my convictions. So I handed the final manuscript over to my editor and said, 'Don't hold back.' Away it went with a degree of trepidation on my part – I wondered if I decided to cancel the whole thing, would I still be able to pull the plug? There followed a period of about four months when the book was with the publisher before it was ready for publication. Four months was a bloody lifetime for me. Jesus, anything could happen with banks, buildings and cash in four months. I was anxious and began to visualise all sorts of nightmare scenarios … launching the book nationally, proclaiming that there is a way forward, that we can overcome this terrible existence that we all find ourselves in and then … a curve ball. A bank moves against me or we run out of cash two weeks after the book is published. It wouldn't have changed what I had written, but it would have been a personal setback that would have required my full attention, notwithstanding having a book published for the first time and possibly having all my financial woes in the public domain as a result. That was my reality and all I could do was get on with things, stick to my guns and have confidence in the fact that if such a curve ball did hit me, I was equipped to deal with it.

In *Shepherd's Pie* I had shared how I had learned to control my fear and execute the start of the fight back. It was a call to arms to all who had been affected by austerity measures or hard-core debt in business, particularly the self-employed, to seek out any and all possible solutions to improve the quality of their business and personal lives, both emotionally and financially. A rallying cry that would possibly incur the ire of bankers, suppliers, customers and creditors. The book would arrive on the shelves of bookshops all over Ireland and maybe be viewed as a test case for moving forward, yet I knew that I had not secured my own future and that the future of my business within the Irish motor trade was still in huge doubt.

I began to waver. How could I launch this book still unsure that my own business would survive or, at the very least, stand before readers and explain with sincerity that my eventual failure was despite my very best efforts? I had stated in the book that I took nothing for granted and that if I were to go down, I'd go down fighting. And I had claimed that I would not stop working on the rehabilitation of my business, not for one minute. So when my publisher called me one morning in August 2011 to tell me that the book was ready to be signed off, a wave of uncertainty hit me. There was no going back from here, they said, was I sure I had no further changes and that I could stand over everything? Oh fuck, I thought to myself. Six months of hard work, now what?

My publisher sensed something was not right. She asked what was troubling me and I said, 'I don't know if I'll still be in business by the time the book hits the shelves because everything is moving and changing daily.' I explained that since I had finished writing a few months earlier I had been concentrating on the future, and that, no matter how I looked at our business in Ireland into 2012 and beyond, I couldn't get our budgets to work. I could see no future in new car sales and I felt that my bank debt would eventually bring us down. I said that I was worried that I could make a fool of myself publishing a book about recovery when my business could still fail. She immediately stopped me and said, 'George, this is your story. This is all about one day at a time. The book clearly demonstrates that your fight has just started, but more importantly, that you're ready, willing and able to fight. Nothing more, nothing less.' She was right. I was willing to fight for my business and livelihood no matter what the outcome, and I had an instant realisation that the launch of the book would be the first shot fired in what would be a war on the isolation and depression experienced by the self-employed as they struggle to survive.

I told the publisher that I was happy with everything and our phone call ended, but I knew at that moment that I no longer had control over what would happen next, how people would see me, my parents, Anne and the business. At a thousand miles an hour everything flashed through my mind – walking down the street in Clonmel after the book was published, the reaction of my kids, the school yard for them, banks, distributors, Revenue and of course my elderly parents. I didn't feel confident, but I knew that it was done, the book was in its final stages and the story would be told.

Later that night, as I was lying in bed thinking about all this, I closed my eyes and made a deal with myself. I decided to leave all the negative thoughts and self-doubt behind me right there and then, and when I woke up the following morning, I would focus on the future, buckle up and enjoy the ride. With that in mind, I chose to make the most of the calm before the storm and have some down time with Anne and the kids, so I went on a ten-day sun holiday, our first since 2008. Business over the summer had been very slow, but virtual sales were showing real promise and more and more of my time was becoming focused on www.wesourceNEcar.com, the online car sales concept I had created in 2010.[1] Nissan and Kia were not fans of my new sales model, believing that it was distracting me from the business of selling new models of their cars. I disagreed. I believe that nowadays there's no such thing for a dealer as selling a new car.

The traditional new car sales model now resembles 'the tail wagging the dog'. When I was learning the ropes in the business I'd persuade a client that they should buy a Nissan over a Toyota for example, based on performance, spec and price. Today customers come to the showroom and tell us which car they want to buy, then inform us of the best price that they have received having visited five main dealers. If I want the sale, I have to beat that best price. (My strategy now is to beat the best price by enough that the client will pay a deposit there and then.) Traditionally, I would trade a Kia for a Kia or a Nissan for a Nissan, but doing that sort of deal each time fills the forecourt with the same makes and models, and that in turn creates a problem with used car sales – if there are buyers in the market for used cars who don't like Kia or Nissan, they won't visit a forecourt that has lots and lots of used Kias and Nissans. Can any business afford to purposely obstruct natural footfall?

---

1   Virtual selling is a sale where the price, mileage, spec, colour and year are agreed on the car that the client wishes to purchase before the dealership source or purchase the actual car.

Then of course there was the link between the franchise distributor in Ireland and their bank. This was a killer for car dealerships because many of the larger distributors in Ireland were controlled by whichever financial institution provided them with funds to buy stock. So the bank dictated how many cars a distributor could stock and, in turn, possibly the same bank would dictate how many cars the dealer could stock and, ultimately, the same bank again would likely provide the finance for the customer who wanted to buy the car! So the banks were a corporate dictatorship in the motor industry. This is why, despite my best efforts to sell both new and used cars the traditional way, I continued to fall deeper in love with the concept of virtual selling and out of love with what had become the jaded motor industry.

Our family holiday was the ideal opportunity to consider 'what next?' Having taken hold of my business finances after my emotional correction in 2009, I now had all of the relevant financial information I needed to make a decision about the future of the business, but felt I needed a push in the right direction.

After the break, and my resolution to hold my head high come what may after publication, I began to feel more excited than anxious about the October launch of the book. Up to the moment when I had signed off on the manuscript, I hadn't shared what I had written with anyone, not even my wife Anne. I needed to write it uninfluenced and alone, but had told Anne, my father and my brother, Brian, that they could read it just before the sign-off deadline – although I know that Anne had sneaked the odd half paragraph up to then! I handed each of them a copy of the manuscript and away they went to read. I always thought that they had shown great courage in allowing me to tell the story considering they all featured so strongly in it, especially my father and Anne. So I was apprehensive about their reactions and the impact it could have on my family. I arrived home from work the following day, just as Anne and my daughter Emily were finishing the book. I wasn't expecting their emotional reaction. There were tears of pride from both of them. My son George was mortified, wondering how it would go down at school, post-launch. Anne said that she would change nothing. She said the story was brilliantly told and that she was so proud. Emily had shed a tear for her granddad, reading how he had quit the job he loved as a result of our business separation. Later my father called me to say that he would support me in every way he could and that he loved the book. He said to have no fear, it would be a best-seller! A call from Brian followed within twenty-four hours, giving me his support. My worst fears were over. I had the support of my family and it was now full steam ahead.

Writing *Shepherd's Pie* was, without doubt, a defining moment for me. I can't imagine that anything else I could do in the future could have such a profound effect on me. It's an undeniable challenge for any person to spend six months reviewing every decision they have made and reflecting on how many of those decisions have impacted so many different lives, often in a negative way. I found the process hugely therapeutic. I came to the conclusion that I had been misguided by ego for some time, believing that I was a better leader or businessman than I actually was. Writing the book and recalling both my successes and failures along the way helped me to get my feet back on the ground. Now I was committed to telling my story of survival and recovery and hopefully making a contribution to someone else's.

Key Lesson: Never be afraid to express yourself. Be prepared to tell it like it is. Don't duck and dive. Always follow your gut instinct. Take time to reflect on decisions, especially any you think were poor, because you will learn more from them. Forgive yourself for past mistakes and move on.

2

Removing the handcuffs

Man cannot discover new oceans unless he has the courage to lose sight of the shore.

André Gide

A common experience in struggling businesses during Ireland's economic collapse was that every time you adjusted, by either further cutting costs or revising down sales projections, you walked away thinking you had solved a problem and so things would surely start to improve – that was certainly my experience. Yet inevitably any positive result was short-lived and only a few months later I would have to make more changes. There was nothing more disheartening than having to react to the constant changes that seemed to be endlessly looming on the horizon – especially when I reached the point where there was nothing left to cut. I had executed changes that you would hope only ever to be forced to make once in any business. I had also fought a succession battle with my father, and the combination of the emotional fallout of that, as well as going from being cock of the walk to dealing with the failure of the business I had fought for control of and facing financial ruin on a massive scale, had led me to picture my own funeral. I was not equipped emotionally or practically to handle this steep descent into despair. However, it was the visualisation of not being here for my kids that spurred me into a more lucid state and ultimately triggered my survival instinct and desire to fight back, to hang in there for them if for no other reason. That emotional correction enabled me to emerge from the despair and face the future with the determination to take action myself and not to allow either the banks or the economy to ruin me beyond any hope of recovery. By mid-2011 I knew beyond all doubt that I wanted not only to survive, but to make a recovery and be successful, albeit on different terms and scale the second time round. But having been bogged down in the mire since 2008, I knew that to do that I would have to knuckle down and do more than just fight for survival. To recover, I would have to reach deeper, I would have to go further to create a functioning business that would earn a living and create a comfortable lifestyle for me and my family.

I love movies. I always have and during the economic crisis, I had taken to watching some of my favourites in bed at night on my laptop with headphones, to help take my mind off the torment of that day. It helped me to relax and unwind, to stop my mind racing and get me off to sleep. One night in the summer of 2011 I was watching *The Untouchables*, starring Kevin Costner and Sean Connery, which tells the story of Eliot Ness taking on Al Capone. In one scene, as Sean Connery's character lies dying from stab wounds, he lifts his head from the floor, grabs the arm of the Ness character and says with passion, 'What are you prepared to do?' It was a plea to Ness to fight fire with fire, to accept that he had to play dirty, because playing by the rules to take down Al Capone would not work. I stopped watching the movie at that point and thought about the various world leaders who faced adversity, how they were challenged and what their response was. I was in the midst of my greatest challenge. How was I going to respond? Would I wilt? Would fear bring me down? More importantly, was I willing to play dirty? What was I prepared to do? I have subsequently asked that same question of many who have sought my help since: how far are you prepared to go to solve your own problems?

Despite our best efforts and the remedial action I had already taken, trading throughout 2011 continued to be really difficult. The only difference was that one of the banks I dealt with (let's call it Bank A) had decided to support the business in February, so we had a fresh injection of working capital, which was vital for our recovery – so many companies around the country need fresh working capital, having burned through any available funds just surviving since 2008. In mid-2010 the bank had taken the very proactive step of introducing me to Advanced Corporate Transformations Limited (ACT). Seán Dunne and Tommy Murphy were ACT, and these two men specialised in dealing with stressed businesses and business owners. Bank A wanted me to engage Seán and Tommy to carry out a root and branch review of the business so that they could help to identify what was required to bring the company back to stability. I reluctantly agreed.

I met Tommy in June 2010. We had a very direct conversation. My strongly held view (which I had no difficulty expressing) was 'Fuck you, you only work for the bank.' Tommy's equally strong response was (not in so many words) 'Fuck you asshole, go it alone if you want. We will work for you, not the bank, and, if you'll let us, I guarantee that we can take you off the bank's radar. We will tear you and your company apart to see what it needs and when we get that figured out, we'll work on figuring out what you need too.' I liked his attitude. I engaged ACT and what followed was a ten-week review of my business and personal life in three steps:

Step One – Was the company viable in the long term?
Step Two – Could I recover from the entire ordeal?
Step Three – Could we raise new working capital?

Within six months we had answered yes to all three and I was committed to moving the business forward and confronting the tough challenges ahead, particularly the considerable debt we were carrying and the fact that the market and general economy still looked very fragile. By mid-2011, ACT instructed me to revise downwards my already conservative projections, because targets were not being met despite my best efforts. The new car market was in tatters and I was forming the view that holding a franchise was counterproductive because a prerequisite for being a franchise dealer was that we had to sustain a certain level of staff. There was also a financial burden in terms of training and technology costs. However, the two biggest issues for me were the level of control over stock held by the banks and the lack of control our distributors had over the supply of stock. Banks were deciding how many cars we should stock as well as when and how we should pay for them, and all to a backdrop of escalating interest costs.

    Tommy, Seán and I sat down and trawled through the books looking for everything and anything related to the cost of holding a franchise. Our review was forensic and possibly something many motor dealers have never done. In our world, holding a franchise was nothing more than a veneer – it made us look good, look professional and competent. The reality is often the opposite and dealers know it, but they don't have an alternative. In my case I was out of options, so when we found that the costs associated with holding a new car franchise exceeded the returns, a very difficult decision had to be made.

Having secured working capital from the bank it was vital not to bleed any further funds, so I had to make a choice between resigning as a franchise dealer and concentrating on www.wesourceNEcar.com or gambling on the Irish economy making a swift and miraculous recovery. Ultimately, the decision made itself, but to qualify it ACT and I broke it down into three simple questions:

a) What causes the most stress for me every day?
    Answer: Distributor and the distributor's financier.[2]
b) What are the projections for captured market share of franchises held over the next five years?
    Answer: Very bleak.
c) Do we have an alternative business model and does that model appear to have a future?
    Answer: Yes.

---

2   Distributors require specific market share, so there was a constant pressure to sell, to register vehicles or to buy stock. We no longer had the firepower to compete to keep them happy but we were still under pressure to perform; we also had to adhere to their very strict criteria for maintaining diagnostic equipment, keeping stock of parts for after-sales service, staff training, etc. This put huge pressure on our cash flow.

The difficult decision was made to resign from Nissan, Kia and Chevrolet, effectively heralding the end of Mordaunt & Sons, and to focus sales efforts on www.wesourceNEcar.com instead. It was a critical decision, taken purely to survive, but ending a twenty-year-plus relationship with Nissan Ireland was tough. It was a partnership that had been started by my father in 1987 and it had played a significant role in my life as I learned the ropes in the business. I knew that the day we removed all of the Nissan signage from the showroom would be particularly tough on Dad and that he would very much see this move as a defeat. We had enjoyed a great working relationship with Nissan Ireland and they had done all they could to accommodate us and keep us as a franchise holder, but we really didn't have any option.

The decision to resign our franchises was a radical step, but it was also a great opportunity to shed costs that continued to drag down the business. Brian Mordaunt & Sons employed a number of our extended family. I now felt that I had only one chance to survive in the motor trade and there would be no second chances. I knew that I would have to confront extended family members who received an income from the business and explain to them that future payments would cease. I saw the parting with franchises as a new beginning and was determined to root out any costs for the new business that didn't enhance its performance, including my own salary, from which I took a sabbatical for eight months and paid myself an industry-standard salesman's salary thereafter. What it meant for the extended family was that we were going our own way and that anything I did with the business in future would benefit only my own or my brother Brian's family. Unsurprisingly, this message was not well received. I really hoped that it wouldn't rekindle the battle between my father and me that had resulted in him leaving the business in 2001. He was unhappy at our decision to resign the franchises and was stunned at the culling of family members. But I was determined to push forward – I had to be and, recalling Connery's line in the movie, I was prepared to do whatever it took to ensure the survival of the business for the sake of Anne, Emily and George. No messing around. I was willing to face down family, distributors, banks or Revenue. I would do anything, including default on loans, make a court appearance, have judgements against me, anything. I had reached the point where I had accepted that nobody would or could save my career except myself, and so emotion and sentimentality had to be removed from the process. I had to believe that my course of action was the best possible one and would release the new business from anything that could hold it back.

By 31 August 2011 we were free from the shackles of franchising and from supporting staff and family who were being paid for historic roles. Financially we were still fragile, but our new business model and related costs were now absolutely transparent. It was a very simple model; buy a car and sell it on at a profit. Our insurance costs fell by fifty per cent overnight because we were no longer stocking so many new cars. Staff numbers were reduced by thirty-five per cent, IT costs were down eighty per cent and we saw a twenty per cent reduction in general administrative costs. Huge overhead costs had been stripped out of the business. Our new business model also meant better margins as we no longer had to do warranty work such as servicing or repairs for half nothing, or waste valuable time listening to endless babble from distributors' sales reps. Within a fourteen-day period we had wiped hundreds of thousands from our overhead base and running costs, and that saving was far greater than whatever we would lose from no longer selling new cars.

I am often asked to list the top five steps I took in the recovery of my business. This was one of them. Being decisive. Instead of stocking new Kias or Chevrolets, which only attracted fans of those brands, we decided to stock a range of sought-after used cars at prices that were competitive. I believe that one of the fastest ways to dig your way out of recession is to find more customers, and, by taking a tough decision, that was exactly what we had done.

The decisions made during the summer of 2011 were difficult and painful, but necessary for survival, and signs were that it was going to work, but I knew there were still some more tactical decisions to be made, including changing banks. While I was receiving tremendous support from Bank A, I thought it would be prudent to start a new relationship with another bank, so I moved any personal funds I had left to a different bank. I had learned the hard way, when my business went from a four-premises dealership in 2007 to one premises with no franchises and a virtual showroom, that having my personal finances in the same institution as my business finances gave the bank far too much visibility and led to ridiculous questions and hassle.

With only a few weeks to go until the launch of *Shepherd's Pie*, I maintained the view that I needed to continue with my street-fighting approach to recovery and survival in business.

I was frantically working to stall the decline, halt our losses and get us back to creating a profit, however small. With the franchises gone, overheads reduced, family payments discontinued and a new bank account, there were only two things left to which I needed to turn my attention. I had to concentrate on making our new business model work, while at the same time confronting the huge issue of my personal-property portfolio, which, as with the majority of property investors in Ireland, had saddled me with huge levels of negative equity. I went back to Seán and Tommy to figure out my next steps, as they had been so insightful and thorough with helping me to see where I could make changes that might yet result in saving my business.

My new operation was dramatically smaller at that stage and, naturally, so was my salary. The costs review had removed all the perks to which I had become accustomed, such as fuel, mobile phone and an inflated salary. I had decided that none of the extravagances that had been acceptable previously would be tolerated after the resignation of the franchises. New beginnings was my motto – as if I had just started a brand-new company. This would ultimately be very positive for the business, but it meant that my earning capacity was so limited that it was becoming impossible to service loans I still had on personal-property investments, another urgent problem to be managed with Seán and Tommy's input.

The issue of debt forgiveness was starting to become a hot topic in the media and in business, but not with banks. All over Ireland, debt was weighing business and business owners down. It was certainly weighing me and my business down, so my next big question was how to deal with it. I wanted to do it with the blessing of the banks that had provided the finance, but I decided that if I failed in my attempts to achieve a level of debt forgiveness or offload the toxic assets, I would deal with foreclosure. I had had enough of the stress and worry that went with trying to service these debts and was determined to change my life, so daily I asked myself the question: what are you prepared to do?

At this point, I was making big decisions to change the course of my life and I recognised that I needed to end the cycle I had found myself in so that I could prepare for the second part of my career in my new business reality. I came to some important conclusions. I refused to continue battling this economy. I refused to live with negative equity for the rest of my life. I refused to spend the next twenty years cleaning up after five unprecedented years of economic meltdown fuelled by a confluence of circumstances over which I had no control and could never have imagined when I committed to the loan repayments. I wanted to find the quickest exit route and get out of the quagmire of debt that I would now never be in a position to repay, no matter what. Due to my exposure to the highest levels of Irish banking in my dealings with ACT, I was becoming increasingly aware that I couldn't just talk about debt forgiveness, I would have to force myself into action. Dismantling our company and resigning our franchises was just the beginning. There was no point moaning about the collapse of my world. I had just started the process of shaping a new one and I was determined to move ahead with this.

I decided that the next step was to secure our business premises. Our building had a very large mortgage and no matter how we worked our budget, we just couldn't service the loan and continue trading. I decided that if we were to avoid any major shocks, we should determine whether we could do our day job from premises other than the main office before approaching the lender. Another tough decision might have to be taken. We had to consider the questions: how relevant is a showroom and display area nowadays, and how much of our forecourt activity is generated from the Internet?

Every customer who contacts us does so by either phone or email or as the result of a walk in. According to our market research, over eighty-five per cent of our enquiries come from Internet searches. The other fifteen per cent come from people browsing our stock when they walk in. Our name was synonymous with the motor industry in Clonmel, so we believed that good marketing, together with a brilliant website and a physical location that gave us ample parking and some office space, would be more than adequate and amount to a third of the cost of servicing the heavy mortgage.

Satisfied that we had a Plan B to propose, we met with the lender and explained that we couldn't service the debt and remain in business. We suggested that, as an alternative to appointing a receiver to our business, they allow us to manage the building on their behalf and to pay rent at market rates for it. This proposal, if accepted, would mean that the bank would avoid the annual cost of both a receiver and security for their asset, as well as the inevitable deterioration and potential vandalism of the building. The over-supply of similar premises in the market ruled out the possibility of a buyer or of securing a new tenant for either the bank or us. But the bank held the deeds and would continue to, so if they had a sitting tenant who could pay rent at market rates while avoiding incurring any cost, they could sit back and wait for the value of commercial property to improve, at which point they could sell. This was an obvious risk for me, as a receiver could have been appointed immediately if things hadn't gone my way on the day, but it was still a win-win proposal as far as I was concerned. It was not an easy decision, but it was a very necessary one to ensure that I could continue trading. I got the result I wanted, but had to be prepared to walk away in order to achieve it, and that had been Plan B. Had that happened, my business would have been completely unrecognisable and I would have had all the bad publicity that goes with having a receiver appointed – that meeting with the bank took place just four weeks before *Shepherd's Pie* was published.

***

In the twelve months that I spent travelling all over Ireland in the wake of the publication of *Shepherd's Pie*, I learned that business people in this country seem to be obsessed with borrowing money or extending overdrafts. It seems to me that this same obsession doesn't apply to research, creativity or development. Very few business owners who I meet take the time to step out of the day-to-day operation of their business to reflect on where they are at personally or in their business, with no distractions. They don't take time to consider their next steps, or time to look to the future and identify potential challenges or opportunities. If you locked yourself away for forty-eight hours with no phone or email, and your challenge was to identify three fundamental changes that would affect you or your company in a positive way, and you met that challenge, it would be time and money extremely well spent. I did it often. I found that it was absolutely necessary for me to step out of the chaos to think and make considered decisions. I believe that I can now anticipate the changes that are coming down the line in the motor industry, so I am preparing myself and my business for them.

While our country has been on its knees since 2008, the rest of the world has moved at a thousand miles an hour. In the five years from 2007 to 2012 we have seen the launch of the very first iPhone and the iPad. We have learned that Apple has a bigger cash reserve than the US government.[3] Could anyone ever have imagined that one business would have more cash in its bank account than Uncle Sam? Smartphone technology has brought rapid change to our business and personal lives, and it is difficult to remember life before email, text, Twitter and Facebook, not to mention Google. Recently I watched a three-year-old boy take his mother's iPhone, key in the passcode, launch an app and start playing a game. In that context, consider these three questions:

1   If that has been the pace of progress in the last five years, what do you think will develop in the next seven?

2   Are you keeping pace and upskilling yourself so that you can work with the generation of kids who are currently in their final year of primary education, who will have finished third-level education in about eight years and arrive in your industry or even business, having grown up with this technology and never known the world without it?

---

3   http://www.bbc.co.uk/news/technology-14340470

3   How will the answer to the first two questions affect the
     future of your business?

Key Lesson: Stop and think. Take time out to assess and take
stock. Spend time away from your business and any distractions
to analyse and make decisions. Remove emotion from your
decision-making process. Once you make a decision, act. Be
bold, be fearless and decide to live or die by the consequences
of your actions to achieve your goals.

3

Spotlight

A good advertisement is one which sells the product without drawing attention to itself.

David Ogilvy

Nine weeks had passed since I returned from our family holiday and so much had happened. I was moving at top speed now, trying to build my new world. Seán, Tommy and I were spending a lot of time together. They were impressed at how I had reacted to their advice and suggestions and I was impressed at what we had collectively achieved. They called me their model student. I didn't see it that way. They showed me an alternative to the chaos and stress that had been my life and I bought into it. They were incredibly efficient and I liked that. They followed through, as I did. They set budgets, I tried to achieve them. We had monthly reviews where they would take no excuses from me and I reported to them as if they were the boss and I was a first jobber. Progress was the name of the game. Despite the challenges that still surrounded me every day in the business, I felt good because we were being decisive and rebuilding. I enjoyed the challenges they presented and they respected my views. Our working relationship became so easy and comfortable that we often found ourselves discussing Ireland and the economy, and what we thought was needed to get it back on track, over a late dinner after an evening's work.

One evening I brought them to see Get Your Locks Off, the barber shop I had opened in 2008.[4] They were impressed with the set up and remarked on the creativity it showed, wondering whether they could tap into my creative side to help other clients of theirs. Needless to say, their business since the start of the recession had been very busy and their entire working week was spent in distressed environments, dealing with people who were on the edge. It must have been very stressful for both of them and sometimes, when I was in their company, I could see the strain.

The publication date for the book was now only days away and I began to prepare myself to move into the promotional phase. I had scheduled twelve weeks from early October to promote the book and now it was time. My story was on the verge of becoming public knowledge. Nerves battled adrenaline, but I wouldn't allow myself to dwell on what was about to happen because, if I stopped and thought for a second about the number of people in my hometown and around the country who were about to become privy to my most private thoughts, I knew I would bottle it. I wasn't afraid of critical analysis, but I was worried about the possible invasion of our

---

4   I had opened this business in 2008, just as the economy was going down-hill, because I spotted a niche market for a barber shop in Clonmel that would be separated from its competition with a little creativity. Get Your Locks Off is a barber shop that offers more than the traditional 'short back and sides' to its young male clientele, allowing them to hang out and play Xbox, Nintendo Wii or Playstation while they wait, or after their haircut, free of charge. It is a visually appealing and entertaining place to be.

privacy and the impact for my family and extended family. But I had committed to doing this and had got the green light from my loved ones, so I got on with it and took comfort in the thought that my story and my family's experience might offer hope or help to another person or family and that, if they did, then as far as I was concerned the book was a great success.

I had to decide what I would and could talk about. The publicist had told me that it would be difficult to secure a slot on the *Late Late Show*, but that we should do our best to get that first and then be ready to travel to the four corners of the country to do all and any radio, TV or print interviews we could get. I would give it my all for the twelve weeks as I wanted to ensure the book earned its place on the shelves for the Christmas market. I had booked a venue in Clonmel to celebrate the launch of the book with a party for friends and family. I was ready.

The Late Late Show team was immediately interested and I went to meet a researcher in Dublin. We had a great conversation and shortly after the meeting I was invited to participate in a show from the audience front row. I would be asked two questions. I would get three minutes and would make the most of them. Fuck it up and I would jeopardise both the book and the message, but get it right and we were out of the traps and away. Saoirse Ronan, The Coronas and Ed Sheeran along with Matt Cooper and Tommy Fleming made up the guest list that evening. Matt Cooper would be discussing his new book *How Ireland Really Went Bust* and it was on the back of that interview that I would be brought in. Anne and the kids were at home waiting for the big moment.

The countdown for the show commenced and then we were live on air. As soon as I saw the first camera sweep past me I knew that *Shepherd's Pie* would shine a spotlight on me, but I had no idea what an emotional journey it would take me on. The marketing campaign for the book was up and running and almost three hours after the show had started, the presenter, Ryan Tubridy, came over to the front row and asked his questions, which I answered with as much passion as I could. As he moved away he said that he must have me over to 2FM (where he hosts a talk radio show) to discuss my story in more detail.

When the show was over, I went back to the green room where I met Matt Cooper. I was booked to appear on his own radio programme a couple of days later, so we chatted for a while and he promised to give me good airtime later that week. A few days later I was interviewed by TV3 and hosted a press launch in Dublin followed by a photo shoot where a renowned chef served me up a bowl of steaming shepherd's pie! Within a week I had appeared on some of the biggest shows in the country. Newspapers were now looking for interviews, as were local radio stations all over the country. Event organisers began to notice me and I was booked for a few speaking engagements, starting with a business expo in Wexford in November. Conor Pope, a journalist with *The Irish Times*, spoke after me at that event. We weren't introduced because of time constraints, so the following night I contacted him on Twitter and we exchanged some pleasantries. That brief exchange later proved to be vital.

It was still very early days for the marketing and promotion of the book and I had of course seen an advance copy, but when a box of books appeared on my desk at work one day, I was like a child on Christmas morning. It would be in bookshops within three days. When I brought copies home I was met with a heartwarming reaction and was so proud of all the work that had gone into it. The dumb asshole who could hardly spell his name at school had written this. Never in a million years had I thought that one day I might be called an author. It was a very proud moment for me to see the finished product sit on the shelf in my living room. Three days later my daughter called me to tell me that she was in Eason's and they had rows of copies of it. She was so excited that she and my son started to hang out in the shop filming with their phones people browsing and purchasing the book. Very cute and very special for me. Tommy and Seán purchased truckloads of the book and asked all of their new clients to read it before they started working with them because they were trying to promote positivity and creativity as part of their message and recovery plans for businesses.

Throughout November 2011 I juggled the day job of continued careful navigation to survival with promoting the new book. I was extremely conscious of decisions that I was making and how they would impact my relationship with the three banks that I was working with. Once there had been four banks on my case, but one seemed to have given up.

I had professional videos made of myself talking about the book and about the general state of the Irish economy and what it was like trying to run a business in such an economy. Within a month of the book launch I had completed over thirty-six interviews in print or on radio and those closest to me had gone from delirious excitement about my being an author to absolute boredom with the entire process. My wife and kids were no longer amused if I appeared on TV, although they continued to ask me how it had gone. My PA and longest serving member of staff, who had stuck with me through thick and thin, would close the door between our offices if she heard me doing an interview, telling me she couldn't listen to it again!

The roadshow continued in this vein for a few weeks but then a shift happened. I began to receive emails from people who had visited the website I had set up just before the book was published (www.georgemordaunt.com), as well as letters from the general public. People called to the office on a daily basis looking to speak to me. This was something that I hadn't anticipated and wasn't prepared for. All of these people were struggling with debt and trauma in some manner, either in their business or personal lives, and wanted to talk, get my advice even. It was a very strange feeling for me as I didn't feel qualified to offer any advice – my business was still not out of the woods and I had debts of €17 million, but the difference was that I had chosen not to allow that to define me. Nonetheless, this was a new dimension in my life and one that would soon gather considerable pace and have a profound effect on me.

The December after the book was published I continued to work with Tommy and Seán on restructuring my business and personal finances as well as staying focused on the heart of my business and trying to sell cars. I was still promoting the book and really enjoying the whole experience. It was quite a roller-coaster ride and I was constantly on the go with one thing or another. I was thriving on the buzz of it all and was a very different man to the one I had been in November 2009 when it had all gotten on top of me. But life has a way of grounding a person. I was driving home one day and my phone rang. I answered and a man introduced himself as being from the *Irish Independent* newspaper. I immediately went into interview-guest mode and felt a thrill that this journalist was calling me about my story. I was brought crashing back to earth when he proceeded to ask, 'Any interest in taking a quarter page advert in next week's paper as we have a sale on at the moment?' Ouch! I politely declined and wished the man a good day. I felt a tad sheepish, but laughed at myself for thinking I was so important for a nanosecond.

Then, around fifteen minutes later, my phone rang again and this time a man introduced himself as being a reporter from Bloomberg TV. I thought to myself, I definitely can't afford an advert on Bloomberg! The reporter asked if I would be willing to film a piece for Bloomberg, in Clonmel, as part of a documentary aimed at a global audience about what austerity was like for people at the coalface in local business. I was delighted and agreed of course, but the first call had taught me a lesson and I didn't take it for granted – you really never know what's around the corner, be it positive or negative.

The Bloomberg piece was followed by another by BBC3, who wanted me to participate in a documentary about Ireland, Greece and Italy and the effects of austerity on business and society. Shortly after the BBC piece, RTÉ called and asked if they could send a crew to film me, the dealership, the barber shop and my wife's business (Anne had opened a boutique in Clonmel in 2005 and while her business was surviving, it was suffering the same fate and shrinkage as most other retailers in the country), covering the story of the recession from a positive viewpoint. They wanted to run the story on the main evening news during Christmas week.

I believe that the interest of the media in me and my story stemmed from two things:

(a) It was relevant to so many people who were lost, who didn't know what to do or who to turn to for help. People from all walks of life, struggling emotionally and financially, could relate to the story.

(b) I had not held back. I had told the whole story and I think that people were relieved to finally hear someone talk so openly about what was really going on, and that made me credible.

Thanks to media interest, my story reached thousands of people one way or another. That resulted in me receiving letters and emails that reduced me to tears in some cases and I felt that while my story was out there, clearly there was a groundswell of people suffering and thinking that they were alone. A few weeks after talking to *Irish Times* journalist Conor Pope on Twitter, I contacted him about the emails and letters I had received. He then wrote a powerful piece in the paper about the trauma that so many small business owners were experiencing, the upsurge in related suicides and the story of *Shepherd's Pie*. That article was the tipping point for the book's message, it now became an international story. The contact I received from people all over the country trebled and my media profile doubled. By mid-December, if it was business, bank or stress related, you couldn't avoid George Mordaunt in the media. As a friend of Anne's remarked during a telephone call one day, 'George is in everything at the moment except the crib!'

That had a knock-on effect on my private life though. Walking down the street or walking into a restaurant in Clonmel was strange. Some people would smile and salute (which I took to mean well done), some would stare (which I reckon meant, 'Why would you tell everybody your business?'), and some would lean across to their companion and whisper (which I took to mean 'Broke my arse, he has the cash stashed'). Yet, however difficult I found it, having made the choice to tell all, it was far more difficult for my wife and parents, who also featured heavily in the book.

By Christmas week RTÉ had aired their piece, headlining on the 6 and 9 p.m. news with 'Clonmel man urges people to stand up to banks'. It was a great high on which to finish the year and what I assumed would be the end of the whirlwind that promoting the book had been, but Christmas would turn out to be nothing more than a break. In the new year invitations continued to arrive for interviews and speaking events. By now, the story was also having an effect on our new business model. The goodwill of many people who read the book began to filter into our enquiry system for cars. They approached us not just because they wanted to buy a car, but also because of the unique concept that was www.wesourceNEcar.com, which they had read about in the book.

Meanwhile, I was still up to my oxters in debt, but it was so far so good with the banks. Then Bank A contacted me and said that they wanted to buy twenty-five copies of the book. They were to be couriered to Dublin where I was told the most senior bank staff had been instructed to read it! The bank wanted to change the way they were communicating with and handling their dealings with distressed customers, and they had decided to use my book as research for their new approach. At a meeting I attended with them in the company of Seán and Tommy a few months later, they explained to me that they had a very clear message they now wanted to communicate. I would learn more about this message in the following months and that meeting was productive and cooperative. But right now the bank had homework to do.

I sat back in my chair gobsmacked when the call ended. Well, fuck me, I thought. You couldn't make it up. A bank that I owed millions to, a bank that I had fought tooth and nail with up to this point, calling me to tell me that my story would be used to help teach bank officials how to treat people who are struggling with respect. In contrast, the bank that had gone silent eighteen months earlier, after I had told them to do their worst but not to call me to threaten my home again, resurfaced. In my opinion, their motivation to do so probably stemmed from all the media attention I had received for suggesting that people should not be afraid of the banks but should instead stand up to them – this bank possibly decided to clip my wings because they didn't like my message and wanted to remind me that neither they nor my debt to them had gone away. During Christmas week they served Brian and me with notice of collection of a loan of over €500,000, giving us seven days to pay before they served us with High Court proceedings. The two banks could not have been more different in their approach – one wanting to move on, assist, partner and learn, the other choosing intimidation. It was the day before Christmas Eve. Ruthless. I thought it was the perfect opportunity to practice what I had been preaching again so, calmly and professionally, I told them to fuck off. I await their response.

***

2011 had been a revelation. I started the year with a business model that was broken and knowing that major changes would need to be made within the year. I knew that the decisions I would have to take would be life-changing for all of us in the Mordaunt family. I knew that I would need to manage these changes not only under the scrutiny of the banks, but also under the spotlight of the media and the general public because of the book. I was fortunate to achieve those objectives and the decisions taken looked as though they would pay dividends. But the one thing I hadn't anticipated or planned for was the depth of the reaction to my story from people all over Ireland, nor was I prepared for how that reaction would affect me. Humility was a relatively new emotion for me, but I now knew that it was an emotion I valued and wanted in my life, and the more emails and letters I received, the more I felt it. It was overpowering. Every day, people contacted me in one way or another, and told me that I had somehow inspired or motivated them and how my story was helping them to change their life. I began to feel emotionally fragile and that came to a head one evening, late at night, when I read an email sent by a man thanking me for helping him to get out of bed that morning and to understand what he had to do.

I have just finished your book. I read it in one sitting. It was utterly powerful. I owe — bank over €1m. My debt has taken its toll on me over recent months, until I read *Shepherd's Pie*. Tomorrow I will get up with a spring in my step to start my fight back and it's all down to you. You have inspired me today George. You have triggered something within me. Now I know I will survive.

Thank you so much from the bottom of my heart. You will never know how much you have helped me today. No looking back from here. Well done and the very best with your book in the future. You deserve every success. You're an inspiration.

I was alone in my kitchen at midnight and when I finished reading, I broke down and sobbed my heart out. I couldn't stop. I was so touched. I hadn't expected or planned to become an inspiration for anyone – I had thought my story might be something some people could relate to and that it might even help some of them, but this was way above anything I had hoped for. However, it was becoming apparent that the attention that the story had been given in the previous twelve weeks had opened the floodgates. I knew that people really needed help on a large scale, and I wanted to be part of the process or system that would help. I had no idea how, but I was motivated. Honesty and openness had gotten me this far. People seemed to respect it. It seemed to me that there was a real desire in Ireland for leaders to cut the crap and just call it as it was. That was going to be my motto. No bullshit. Call it as it is, no matter how uncomfortable that discussion might be.

Key Lesson: Don't be afraid to share your story. Talking to somebody can sometimes lead you to taking the first steps needed to begin recovery. Talking, sharing, expressing yourself, planning and communicating are all fundamental in the process of recovering from any distress in life.

4

Humbled to tears

Humility is nothing but truth, and pride is nothing but lying.

St Vincent de Paul

In 1992 I attended a meeting called by Nissan Ireland, where eight or nine motor dealers were invited to discuss marketing initiatives with them. It was a fairly common practice and happened about three times a year with the sole objective of improving sales of Nissan cars in Ireland. Dealers were asked to share their opinions and experiences on different issues. I remember that after that particular meeting I was called aside by one of the senior managers at Nissan, who 'suggested' to me that I might consider an alternative tone, perhaps a less direct approach, during discussions on certain subjects. I was about twenty-five years old at the time and obviously what I lacked in maturity and experience I made up for in confidence! But his advice stuck with me. Of course I now understand that he was delicately telling me to shut the fuck up on sensitive subjects that should (apparently) never be discussed in a public forum.

That mindset still exists – that there are some things that should not be discussed openly. Even journalists are often told what subjects will be discussed prior to press conferences and if anybody strays from the directive there are usually consequences. It makes me wonder about what really constitutes freedom of speech. There are many Irish people who refuse to buy into this trend – Eamon Dunphy has made a career out of it, Roy Keane and Bob Geldof are just two more who come to mind, and I have a tendency towards it myself. Some people think of it as wearing your heart on your sleeve, but if I am asked a straight question I will answer it honestly and without embellishment, even if it's a personal question. I believe that it was the honesty with which I told my story in *Shepherd's Pie* that triggered the release of emotion from people who read it and led to so many of them writing to me to share some very personal thoughts and experiences, possibly for first time outside their private sphere. Some of the stories were terribly sad and the more I read and listened, the more I could see the real, human cost of economic failure – the true cost of austerity – the more troubled I felt.

What follows are a few examples of the emails and letters I received, and they demonstrate clearly the terrible issues that many Irish people face in today's economy. Elements of the letters have been changed to protect the identity of the original writers.

> As a young man I had the awful trauma of having to identify the body of my father who had taken his gun and used it to shoot himself. He did so because he owed a lot of money to his bank. The farm that he left behind then became my focus in life. Over the years that followed I assumed responsibility for the running of the farm.
>
> With some modest success during the late nineties I

decided to branch out by investing in property. Nothing enormous, just two rental properties. I also opened a small business. I enjoyed some more success. I invested in the farm and purchased a small retail unit having had a successful start to my business. I enjoyed the late years of the Celtic Tiger boom; however, all of that quickly came to an abrupt end when the banks decided to carry out what they called a 'root and branch' review of my assets as a result of the collapse of the property market. That was 2009. Now I am fast approaching the end of 2011 having lost almost everything. The business is finished. The farm has a charge on it from my bank. They are being really aggressive. The two houses have no tenants. The retail unit is only generating rent of €14,000 annually against a mortgage repayment of over €85,000 a year. The pressure has become overwhelming. I owe a total of €1.8 million. I am months in arrears on my own mortgage. I have no income. I have tried to come to an arrangement with the banks but they are not listening to me. They have no respect and no understanding of what I am going through. I feel so down. My father is on my mind so much that it worries me. My wife asked me to get some help. I have but it's doing little good.

The other night I started to read your book. I could relate so much to what you were going through. Our stories are so familiar. I read the first half in one sitting. It was late at night. I turned off my light but couldn't sleep. After 4 a.m. I got up and while sitting in a seat overlooking my garden I decided that I needed to do something to look after my family. I found myself thinking of what I could do … eventually planning my own death so my wife could cash in on a policy that I have. Having worked all of it out in my head I stood up and walked to the cabinet that had the gun that my father used. Suddenly I stopped, remembering a technical point that needed to be addressed for my wife. This needed to be sorted before I could carry out my plan. I couldn't believe what I was thinking, George, but in a weird way it gave me some relief knowing that they would be all right. I knew it would take me a few days to sort out paperwork so I stalled on my plan.

Since then I finished reading your story. It has given me real hope that I can recover and for that I thank you. In some way it has created some emotional energy. I know that sounds weird, but after finishing it I thought that perhaps there is something to fight for. You are to be commended for such bravery and honesty. Your story has helped me greatly. I would love to come and meet you. If you could advise me on the next steps that I need to take I would be really grateful. I feel terribly stressed at the moment but at the same time I feel that I am ready to start fighting back. Thank you for writing this wonderful story. It has made a great difference to me.

*

I desperately need to help my brother. My daughter bought your book as a Christmas present for him but he has not read it yet. He had a very successful business which he sold in 2005. He then went into property. Now he is in financial ruin – high borrowings, bank debt, huge interest repayments, lost his family and his health is suffering as a result. I think you know his pain.

He left Ireland last year to start a new life abroad, but things are not working out for him. He feels he will never get a decent job at his age and is very depressed and desperate to start all over again, but with the banks at his heels, the pressure is huge.

I am a strong person and very mindful of the pitfalls. I am also very optimistic and positive, but I just can't come up with any advice that might work for him in this economy and I want to help or get help for him, but where do I start? Our families and friends are all in the same boat and it's relentless doom and gloom, with companies and businesses closing every week.

Any suggestions as to how I can help my brother overcome the horrible past that went so wrong for him and help him see a wonderful future ahead?

*

I really admire your efforts in getting yourself out of a terrible financial position. I am in a similar situation and would really appreciate some advice/pointers in relation to dealing with the banks, etc.

I have run a retail business for the last nine years. A few years back I bought a building and after a long and expensive planning process developed it into retail units and apartments. I depended heavily on my family to support my investments – support that included personal guarantees. Unfortunately my father has since passed away. We miss him terribly and now the bank is looking for new guarantees, which we are not ready or able to give them as our situation has changed greatly. I need to renegotiate millions of pounds of debt with a view to holding onto my parents' property if at all possible. I would be very grateful for any advice you would have as a result of your own experience.

*

I was overwhelmed by these letters and emails, and felt very uncomfortable when people said that I had inspired them, because I saw myself as nothing more than a dumb car salesman who, even in a time of crisis, couldn't keep his bloody mouth shut. But it felt like *Shepherd's Pie* had become the story of the recession and I started to feel almost a sense of responsibility. I discussed how I was feeling with Anne and she told me not to forget that, regardless of my coming clean about our collapse and the recession, the story was full of hope because it was also a story about acceptance and recovery. People who are depressed, worried sick and fearful need inspiration and it seems I represented that for many. I began to sense a change in my personality. Even on a night out with friends, when everyone was relaxed and enjoying themselves, I felt weighed down. I had read so many awful stories, met so many people asking for help – I felt helpless but compelled to do something. I just couldn't figure out what.

I shared what I was feeling with Tommy over a few drinks one evening and described how emotional I was feeling daily. He could relate to it because his job exposed him to much the same on a daily basis. He told me that one of ACT's clients had told him that if it hadn't been for their work with him, he would have committed suicide. It would take a heart of stone not to be affected by that. We were both seeing first-

Humbled to tears

hand that many people were lost and in need of direction, and we pondered ways that we might join forces to help. What a privilege it would be, to be able to effect change in somebody's life. The next day we agreed that while it would be wonderful to find a way of helping people, our aspirations to change the world were influenced by one too many glasses of wine and left it there. But time would prove us wrong.

Two days later my office phone rang at 9 a.m. A woman's voice. 'Is that George Mordaunt?'

I confirmed that it was and she said, 'I just want you to know that you are the most amazing man.' Silence. I didn't know what to say. Then I heard her quietly sobbing.

'Are you under pressure? Which bank is it?' I asked.

She told me. The bank she named had featured heavily in some of the horror stories I had heard. All these stories were consistent in their criticism of how this bank was communicating with its customers. This lady was recovering from illness. She had lost her business and investment properties to a receiver and had just been served with a twenty-one-day eviction notice from her home. She was in a state of flux. She told me that her husband was a good man in a very good job, but he just didn't know how to handle it. She asked me if she could come to Clonmel to meet me for a chat.

A few days later we met at my office and talked for over two hours, by which time I could see that she had not engaged with the bank. She was not doing enough to keep them informed. As time was against us because of the eviction notice, I drafted Seán and Tommy in to help. I urged the lady and her husband to engage the services of ACT, which they did. To cut a long story short, Seán and Tommy identified the

51

problem and offered a solution that the couple presented to the bank; it was accepted within weeks.

This was a small victory that I had helped to achieve and it felt good. It then occurred to me that, together, we had accomplished what we had babbled about a few nights earlier – we had effected a positive change in someone's life. I wondered if we could do more of this. Anne had been right – I started to believe that my story could offer hope, inspiration and motivation. The experience was changing me in ways I never expected. I felt a bizarre mix of confidence and humility. Well, that is, I thought that what I was feeling was humility but wasn't sure, so I googled it! One set of search results listed three qualities that define a humble person: listen more than you talk, use the response 'I'd be honoured', say 'it's my pleasure'. That seems quite false to me. I believe that humility forms part of your personality – you either genuinely have it or you don't. Sometimes, you appear humble but don't necessarily feel it, especially in business. However, this was a trait that I now recognised within myself, and I realised that as a result people were interacting with me in a far more expressive and honest way. The Australian writer John Dickson said, 'Humility intensifies credibility'. I was finding this to be true and with that credibility came an enormous sense of responsibility and a desire to do better and change what I could.

I was also aware that interest in me and my story would eventually wane, so I was considering how I could continue to assist and offer the benefit of my experience once this period of my life was past. Throughout the flurry of promotional activity around the book, I had continued to work with the banks trying to manage the massive debts that I had. The guys from ACT and I met every month to review my position with the banks. I was in constant communication with all of the banks but one about my debt and how to resolve it, and eventually we started speaking openly to them about some kind of write-down. The banks made it very clear that they would listen to a common-sense approach, which, in my view, suggested that some element of debt forgiveness was the way forward, but that idea was knocked back immediately. They informed us that there was no formula to apply such action and that they were far from being able to even consider that idea. However, I was €17 million in debt. I couldn't service even half of it and could see no way that I would ever be able to. Surely something had to give.

In a discussion with Bank A it became clear that there was a considerable difference between debt forgiveness and debt write-off (as described in Chapter Seven). I was given a very swift education on the difference between the two and told that I qualified for neither. The bank expected me to make every effort to continue to service all of my debt, but there was a tiny chink in their armour, which was the suggestion that if a policy on this issue was to be forthcoming, I'd be the first to know, provided I continued to service my existing debt as best I could and keep communications open. OK, I thought to myself, there's still some hope for the future. We'll come back to this again, all hope is not lost.

Since I had met Seán and Tommy, they had not just educated me on how to improve in my business but, more importantly, they were giving me the education of a lifetime on how to work with banks. Meetings were held at the desks of the bank managers, where I witnessed how they were running their affairs while working out their own road map to recovery. What I was seeing and hearing was incredible, and it was information that I wanted to share with those distressed people who had contacted me after the book was published. The ACT guys also recognised a sea change in their dealings with the banks, as these institutions went through the process of recapitalisation and nationalisation. They seemed now to be obeying very clear instructions from their boards to change course and follow a new path in the attempt to bring about permanent improvement in their balance sheets. These were amazing times to be sitting at a senior bank official's desk, especially when you owed them the amount of money that I did. I had come full circle.

As the phone calls and emails in response to *Shepherd's Pie* continued to roll in, I tried to reassure people and give them hope that things would eventually change. Not many believed me. So many people were still gripped with fear. They were still in a state of flux. I was both chuffed and humbled by it all and was delighted to see the banks starting to get their act together. Perhaps my going public with my story had done some good. That was it for me. That was the push I needed. I still wasn't clear what it was that I could do, but I decided that I would act, and resolved to know how by January 2012. I had a goal and my deadline was set. I would take a break over Christmas and think about it. During the holidays I decided to set up Insight – a one-to-one advisory service. My advice would not be supported by a paper qualification but would be offered in layman's terms based on my own experience. That was it. It wouldn't be the technically or legally sound advice of an accountant or solicitor, but the advice of somebody who had gone through a traumatic process of restructuring and making dramatic lifestyle and business changes themselves. Based on the feedback I had received, I believed that there would be a huge appetite for such a service. For bigger or more intricate or complex cases for which I was not in a position to advise, I planned to refer clients to Tommy and Seán. We had figured out a way of passing on what we were learning at the highest levels of Irish banking. We were all in agreement. For 2012, Insight and ACT would set a goal to effect change in the lives of people struggling with any form of debilitating debt.

Key Lesson: Never fail to understand that the first step to your recovery is to ask for and accept help. Pride isn't an excuse.

5

Shepherd's Pie Ingredients

It's not necessary to change. Survival is not mandatory.

W. Edwards Deming

I have been very vocal over the last few years about how we as a country can be proud of having put our hands into our pockets to bail out what we thought were Irish banks. We stepped up and acted based on the information to hand, but the goal posts have changed over the years that followed and we haven't reacted. I think that we should be ashamed at our lack of response and action as a population since then, especially at the suggestion that we may have taken one for Europe so that contagion in the banking sector in the Eurozone would be avoided.[5] As a people, the only expression of our anger has been the way we removed Fianna Fáil from governing us. Other than that we have done nothing. A moan here and there, a bitch about recession, a swipe at politicians, but little else. No mass protest. No sit in. No rising up of any

---

5   http://www.telegraph.co.uk/finance/financialcrisis/8937224/Heroic-Ireland-can-do-no-more-it-is-up-to-Europe-now.html

heroes on this occasion. During the Ulster Bank IT fiasco of 2012, I heard on national radio that, by 2 July, some two weeks into the trouble, only two people had complained to the ombudsman. Why are we so apathetic as a nation?

Over the last twenty years there have been crises that resulted in defining moments in many countries and, generally, one or more individuals have emerged and inspired the people. A good example is Russia in June 1991, when Boris Yeltsin was elected. The anti-communist candidate, Yeltsin showed no fear – motivated and inspired by Russians en masse, he stood on a tank to address hundreds of thousands of people at the Kremlin despite huge security concerns. Or the utterly fearless Tank Man, the young man who stood before a moving tank in Tiananmen Square in 1989. A Google search for 'political uprisings in the last twenty years' returns results including the Los Angeles riots and Tiananmen Square in the top three, but number four is Greece because of the Greek people's protests and expressions of anger at their government's austerity measures. Greece received a seventy per cent reduction on their debt in March 2012 – could the decision taken by those bond-holders (mostly banks) have been influenced by the riots?[6] It is impossible to know for sure, but Ireland has done nothing in response to austerity measures and to date has received no concessions. Draw your own conclusions. We have no Tank Man, no hero, no leader – while there have been individual responses, such as the 'Anglo Avenger',[7] there has

---

6   http://www.reuters.com/article/2012/02/21/us-greece-idUSTRE8120HI20120221

7   http://www.independent.ie/national-news/courts/storming-the-gates-2359024.html

been no mass protest, no rallying call, and by accepting these measures, we have effectively consigned the task of picking up the pieces to the next generation. Our reaction as a country is unforgivable, yet we will probably continue not protesting and not demanding to be heard, bitching and moaning to each other over the national airwaves on issues that are meaningless in the greater scheme of things.

The introduction of the household charge was a typical example of this. We spent from January until March 2012 debating the rights and wrongs of it and claiming we weren't going to pay it. In the same month it was introduced, Greece walked away with that massive reduction in its debt while, at exactly the same time, we decided to sell our state assets in order to reduce our debt. It beggars belief but it is fact. Talk about taking a kicking. I find the whole situation incredibly frustrating. Having fought to survive in 2008, trying to initiate recovery in 2009 and hanging on by a thread until 2010, hoping for and expecting growth in 2011 and beyond, we found ourselves facing the possible end of the Euro and watching Italy, Spain and Cyprus sail towards bailouts to a backdrop of deeper European recession and further austerity.[8] I think it is fair to say that by 2012 some of the biggest countries with the largest economies in Europe had begun to experience what Ireland had struggled with in 2008.

Despite all the positive steps I had taken over the last couple of years, in early 2012 the worsening news from Europe brought back that helpless feeling of 2008 – I began to wonder if anything I had done would actually make a

---

8   http://www.finfacts.ie/irishfinancenews/article_1021441.shtml

difference. I felt that if the EU was to fail, then Ireland would have no chance of recovery. I couldn't see hope in the economy, the government, Europe or the banking sector. I could see mass emigration and recession fatigue across the country. In fact, the sight of Enda Kenny telling us that we would pay our way no matter what, prompted me to start wondering whether I should consider emigration.[9] Could I leave, and, if I did, what would the implications be? What steps would I need to take to wind things down so we could go? How would Anne feel about it? How would it affect my children? We would all need to start over and that could be tough on them, but if we were to leave we would head for Canada, with its strong economy, four definite seasons, fantastic education and healthcare systems and the chance of a future for the kids. It would be a bold move and I asked myself, if I were a good parent and thought only of my kids, would I be doing the right thing in the long run by moving them to Canada? While it might be tough at the start, it could be seen as being cruel to be kind – I would be removing them from a society where 'on the piss, wear your pyjamas to the shop to get a jumbo breakfast roll' seems to have become an accepted part of life. Canada offered an attractive alternative and I seriously thought about it, to the extent that I discussed the possibility with Anne. Ultimately, we decided against it. Maybe I wasn't tough enough. I think deep down Anne would have gone for it if I had had it in me to make the move. So, having decided to stay put, I had to figure out a way to make this life, and our

9   http://www.independent.ie/national-news/kenny-we-will-continue-to-pay-our-way-3000388.html

future, worth continuing to fight for. Life had to be worth living. I couldn't keep struggling indefinitely.

For a while my outlook was as bleak as it had been during the week in 2010 when the then leader of the country had allegedly been hung-over during an interview on national radio, and this had been followed by his party's untrue denial that our country was being bailed out by the EU/IMF/ ECB Troika.[10] I decided that, once more, I was on my own. I felt abandoned. I felt let down by my country. It's not an exaggeration to say that I felt like the entire country had been wiped out by some kind of disaster and only my family and I were left, so it was up to me to do whatever I needed to do to gather food and survive. No joke, that's how alone I felt.

Imagine living in Haiti after the earthquake in January 2010. Imagine if you and your family survived and having had no food or water for days, you found yourself in a compound when a UN lorry arrived to distribute bread and water, but everybody knew that there wouldn't be enough to go round. For me the banks were that lorry, cash was the food and water and the person distributing it was the system or the government. How would you approach that lorry? Would it be in the apathetic Irish way, would it be with grace and manners letting others go before you, or would you fight tooth and nail, doing anything you had to do to ensure you got enough to feed your family? I know what I would do in an extreme survival situation. I would fight brutally and deal with the consequences afterwards.

Just to be clear, I'm not comparing the collapse of the Irish economy or my business with the horror of a natural disaster,

---

10   http://www.rte.ie/news/2010/1114/okeefeb.html

but simply using the analogy to describe how I felt at that point. I could relate to the late Brian Lenihan's despairing description of his experience of signing the deal:

'I have a very vivid memory of going to Brussels on the final Monday and being on my own at the airport and looking at the snow gradually thawing and thinking to myself: this is terrible. No Irish minister has ever had to do this before,' he says [*sic*]. 'I had fought for two and a half years to avoid this conclusion. I believed I had fought the good fight and taken every measure possible to delay such an eventuality and now hell was at the gates.'[11]

It appeared that the government couldn't fix the Irish economy and I would have to continue to do whatever it took to survive. I decided that what I needed to do to get back to a more positive place was to actively push on with the plan I had come up with in 2010 to get my life back on track.

When I had made the decision in 2010 that I wanted a better-than-this existence for my family, I started to think on my feet. I decided I would stop at nothing to find my way back to some quality of life. I would break every rule on the way if I had to, and to hell with what anyone thought. I needed a firm strategy to move forward, so I sat down and asked myself: what would I need to do in order to own my recovery? What were the obstacles blocking my recovery? Those issues needed to be identified and dealt with. I took seven items: a cup, a phone charger, a DVD case, a key ring, a letter opener, a pencil

---

11   http://www.bbc.co.uk/news/uk-northern-ireland-13181082

and a ruler. On each item I stuck a tab on which I wrote what the item represented, each being one of the obstacles to my recovery and, therefore, to living a life of quality again. My method might look and sound a bit crazy, but it worked for me and was a simple way of breaking the larger problem into manageable chunks – defining the individual challenges to address in order to solve the bigger problem. The issues that I identified were:

1   Fragile emotional state. Exhaustion, fear and pride.
2   Personal finances, providing for my family.
3   Financial state of the business.
4   Level of debt.
5   Banks, what they wanted, what I could give them, what they might do.
6   If number three failed, what was Plan B for earning a living?
7   The fallout legally, financially, emotionally if I failed to resolve the first six issues.

From this list of seven, I was able to identify three major problems that were at the root of everything. If I could address these, life would be worth living again:

1   Debt
2   Insolvency
3   Plan B

Debt related to the banks and the pressure they were putting on me. It was about servicing unrealistic debt levels, most of which were attached to properties that no longer carried much value, such as a commercial loan of €400,000 on a property now worth €100,000 and falling. No matter what I did, it would be at least two decades before I could hope to see any return from these properties, either from rent that would service the repayment or from a sale to clear the loan, and even if I wanted to hang on in there for that period of time, I couldn't get a bank to support any long-term plan.

Insolvency. My balance sheet that was totally upside down as a result of the crisis and some very poor professional advice I had taken. It was clear that it would take years to recover, if it was possible at all. I take the view that this is distinctly different to debt, because the debt was incurred when I could service repayments with my income from a thriving business, so, now that the business was insolvent, I could service neither my personal nor the business debt.

Plan B. What was it? How would I earn a living? Wasn't that the only relevant issue? Weren't health and happiness more important than anything else?

This brings me to the question that I have probably been asked the most since I went public with the story of the collapse of my business – the 'what did you do to recover' question. My answer might be disappointing. I didn't reinvent the wheel. I didn't come up with a master plan. Having finally arrived at my list of three key problems, I decided to start again. That was it. Start all over again in the business but learn from my mistakes and create a new business model. I still wanted to be in the business. I enjoyed it, but this time I knew it would have to be done differently. I couldn't sort out my debt problem as it stood, because it was simply too large for me to deal with.

Likewise, I couldn't deal with potential insolvency because the balance sheet of the business was beyond redemption and that was also outside my control. I could, however, come up with Plan B. That was my lifeline. I wanted to trigger my very own 'Chapter 11', which is a concept I really believe in. In America, if you go bankrupt you can file for Chapter 11 of the Bankruptcy Code, which permits reorganisation of a business under the bankruptcy laws and is available to every business, sole trader or corporation, as well as individuals.[12] It offers a number of mechanisms to restructure business finance and loans on more favourable terms, by giving new lenders first priority on the earnings of the reorganised business; this means that lenders present under the old regime are de-prioritised. This allows you to borrow more money to continue in business with effectively a clean slate, with the intention of recovering sufficiently so that you can eventually repay the original lenders too. The bankrupt person is then entitled to emerge from the bankruptcy filing twelve months later and allowed to start all over again.

During the global economic crisis there have been some of the biggest Chapter 11 moments in US history, such as Lehman Brothers, who filed for bankruptcy in September 2008 holding over $600 billion in assets. Days later Barclays acquired part of Lehman's, which included the bank's midtown Manhattan skyscraper. Lehman's Chapter 11 filing remains the biggest ever in US corporate history and,

---

12   When a business is unable to service debt or pay its creditors, the business or its creditors can file with a federal bankruptcy court for protection under either Chapter 7 or 11. For more information see http://www.uscourts.gov/FederalCourts/Bankruptcy/BankruptcyBasics/Chapter11.aspx

although Lehman Brothers has failed to emerge in the same format or structure that it had before,[13] there have been other examples of how the Chapter 11 process can offer very creative solutions. Chrysler filed for bankruptcy with $39.3 billion in assets in April 2009 only to emerge restructured and functioning forty-one days later.[14]

The most creative example of starting over using Chapter 11 in my view, was carried out by General Motors, which remains the largest automotive company in the world. A dramatic slide in revenue in 2008 forced the company to file for bankruptcy in June 2009. The US government then provided practical financing, which allowed GM to emerge from bankruptcy in July 2009. By November it was re-listed on the NYSE with an Initial Public Offering of $20.1 billion. The US government still owns twenty-seven per cent of the company, but it is functioning, making money and creating employment.[15] If Ireland had a similar system, what a difference it would make. But instead, Irish business owners try to slink away to the UK in order to seek bankruptcy on terms that offer some hope of a second chance.

Those two words became my mantra – second chance. Why shouldn't I have one in my business? Chapter 11 wasn't available to me so I decided to create it for myself. That was it. I would force it if I had to and was prepared to do whatever it took, no matter what.

13   http://dealbook.nytimes.com/2012/01/10/lehman-still-doing-deals-in-a-second-life-on-wall-street/

14   http://www.msnbc.msn.com/id/30489906/ns/business-autos/t/chrysler-files-bankruptcy-protection/#.UIbtTK73CYI

15   http://www.nytimes.com/2011/06/08/business/08gm.html?_r=0

First up from my list was to find an acceptable way of dealing with the issue of debt. I went to Banks A and C, with whom I had a proactive relationship and, with the help of Seán and Tommy, demonstrated mathematically and with absolute sincerity that I was exposed to an approximate €10 million-plus black hole of negative equity across different properties, both commercial and residential. Furthermore, we compiled a report confirming that this balance would increase if action wasn't taken immediately. This had already been demonstrated by the fact that three years earlier I had suggested that I should try to sell properties for around €1 million that today would only get approximately €700,000 on the market, thereby leaving a much higher residual debt than would have been the case had the banks taken any initiative or shown either leadership or longer-term vision back then. To avoid further losses, we suggested that I should commence a programme of asset disposal. I would proactively set about selling each property, returning to the bank with firm offers, if they came in, to seek their approval before completing any sale. This would crystallise the bank's loss and leave me facing significant loans without any assets to back them up. But taking this action would therefore force a conclusion – I would mathematically prove that if I couldn't service the debt with the assets, it certainly couldn't be serviced without them, so the bank would have to make a commercial decision as to how to proceed, especially bearing in mind that they were now underwritten by taxpayers' money.

Next on my list was insolvency, or the trading entity that was Brian Mordaunt & Sons. It had become very clear to me that, despite the enormous help of Bank A, I was not going to be able to salvage the business in its current format and would incur more debt if I continued to trade. I had accepted that the investment required to run a new car franchise versus the return was no longer viable, particularly given the continuing decrease in the number of new car sales. Moreover, I no longer had the necessary financial firepower to drive the business at a level that would be required for success, so the best I could hope for was to limp along for the next decade. Limping along only heightened the stress. Therefore, my decision was that elements of our business should cease to trade. I had tried everything to make it work and the bank could see that because the lines of communication with them were open. I had been educated to understand that the only way to engage with the bank was with frank and open discussions. No cute hoor stuff. Ceasing to trade was painful. However, with the cessation came the elimination of large parts of the business debt to Revenue and the banks – I understand that not paying Revenue has a knock-on effect throughout the economy, but my intention was to ensure that no private business to whom I owed money went unpaid, and that was at the cost of both bank debt and missed payments to Revenue. I maintained an open dialogue with Revenue to ensure that if at all possible all monies, including penalties, would eventually be paid, and continued to engage with the banks with the intention of ultimately settling my debts with them too. Those meetings with the banks were very difficult and very painful. It was a self-declaration of failure in one sense, but on the other hand, it was a brave and rational decision to take in order to try to move forward.

Finally to the last item on my list, creating Plan B. A company isn't a living creature. A balance sheet doesn't have a soul. It isn't real. However, in my case, it represented thirty years of hard graft by my father, brother and myself. I felt desperately sad about its imminent failure, despite my resolve to do whatever it took to survive. I was acutely aware that my father was looking on from the wings at the fate of his life's work.

When I told my parents what I had decided to do, my mother became very upset. Our brief discussion ended with me barking aggressively at her for what I felt was a reaction that heaped more pressure on me. In hindsight, I don't think that I explained what I was doing very well, and so I think she saw it as immediate unemployment for my brother Brian and me, as well as the end of the family business. I tried to explain to my parents that their life's work, as well as my twenty-five-year career in the business, weren't represented by a franchise or by a balance sheet. Our combined efforts over the last thirty years were defined only by our name and its unbreakable link to the motor industry in Clonmel. The Mordaunt name was synonymous with offering customers a quality service and represented trust, experience, knowledge and credibility, and that would be protected. With our new business model, Brian and I would ensure that the Mordaunt expertise and knowledge would survive in the industry in Clonmel and that the Mordaunt brand would not cease to exist. We would continue with the name 'Mordaunt Group' and start again; however, this time we would go back to our roots and strip out all the politics of new car franchising and get back to offering the same service that had started the business some thirty years before – quality used cars, but sourced and marketed in a twenty-first-century way, offering

Ireland's first virtual car sales model in www.wesourceNEcar. com. It would be the perfect blend of our car-selling heritage mixed with modern technology and driven by our creativity. I believed it would be a successful business, the light that would get us out of the horrible darkness that had consumed our family. We were united for the first time in ten years.

In *Shepherd's Pie* I set out the basic day-to-day steps that I was taking to keep creditors at bay, while introducing simplified procedures and getting back to the heart of the business myself so I could maintain a tight grip on profitability. I continued to use that method when running the new business and then turned my attention back to my debt problem. All of the assets of Brian Mordaunt & Sons were for sale. The old family business had died and the foundations were laid for the next phase of the Mordaunt Group to continue trading in the Irish motor industry. The tough decisions had been made and I knew that the final part of this journey would be to see what the fallout was going to be. I had no guarantees from the banks that they would write off or write down any of the remaining debt, but the lines of communication were open and positive. I had a good relationship with Bank A and they could see that I was being proactive. They weren't constantly chasing me, seeking answers. They weren't being supplied with sloppy information and I wasn't promising anything on which I knew I couldn't follow through. In many cases like my own, the banks had simply appointed receivers, and I suspect that resistance to supplying information or poor communication might have contributed to that decision. My relationship with the banks now was the total opposite and I had avoided receivership to date. With the help of ACT, I had been convinced and could see for myself how the only way to have productive discussions with the banks was with openness, and that any information I provided had to be polished and perfectly accurate. That way, the banks could see a credible proposal backed up with a willingness to act.

I think that was the most important step in my recovery because this approach offered the hope of achieving a satisfactory end for all parties, without fear, confrontation or aggression. Once I had been terrified, but now I had no fear because I knew that no matter what, I would look after my health, my family and my home. I had prioritised them. I had a fire in my belly to fight for survival and Tommy had helped me to harness that into positive but firm communication with my banks and creditors. Once, people would ask me, why would you get rid of the 'new cars' part of your business? Or, why are you selling houses now when the market is depressed? Are you mad? Eventually the most asked questions became, how did you get past where you were? How did you extricate yourself from the mire? How do you cope with the pressure? Having met so many people in trouble, I knew that my position wasn't so different from many others. Here is a typical scenario:

Jack owns a computer software business which has been operating for about eighteen years. While business was good, he decided to buy two investment properties to rent out, each costing €235,000, which he is currently repaying on an interest-only basis. The houses are currently valued at just €135,000 each. He also bought a site for €140,000 where he had intended to build his dream home. The site is currently valued at €34,000. When he purchased the site, his home had equity, but now he is in negative equity with a mortgage of €275,000 on a house valued at €240,000. Borrowings on the investment properties are static at €470,000 with current values of just €270,000, leaving a negative balance of €200,000. His business has an overdraft facility of €20,000 which never drops below €16,000 and frequently reaches €19,800, leaving Jack sweating it out often, hoping his cheques don't bounce. His business is in arrears with Revenue and he has a twenty-four-month payment plan agreed to resolve that. The bank has registered a charge on the two investment properties and the site, and Jack has had to give a personal guarantee for the loan on the site. Because the site formed part of his plan to build the dream house, he also used his home to secure the site purchase. The business has seen a thirty-five per cent reduction in turnover in the last three years. The reductions combined with a bad debt write-off (forced because some of his clients went to the wall) have forced cuts in staff numbers. Jack's income has also reduced by over thirty per cent. As a result his mortgage has slipped into arrears by three months. His balance sheet shows his business to be insolvent.

His bank wants to stop the business overdraft and at the same time switch the loans on the investment houses back to interest and capital instead of interest only. The site loan is due for review and the bank has indicated that unless increased security is given they will call in the loan, as Jack has failed to make any payment on the site in the last eight months. On top of this, his accountant won't sign off on the annual accounts because of the balance sheet. This month's taxes are due but Jack can't make the repayments on the payment plan as well as fund the current taxes. He has an unfair dismissal charge from a former employee due to be heard within the next four months and to cap it all off, he is locked into a twenty-year-upwards-only lease agreement on the premises from where he runs his business – which is also one month in arrears. Yesterday he lost his best client because the client was dissatisfied with the level of service received from Jack's company.

There are hundreds and possibly thousands of people facing a similar situation all over Ireland, and their typical day includes dealing with financial debts and the misery that goes with them. The pressure is severe and the fear is even worse. Jack is fire-fighting but hoping for what? A miraculous recovery in the economy or in property prices? Is he hoping for the banks to change their mind about their demands? A comprehensive Statement of Affairs detailing Jack's position on both his personal and business finances is outlined in the Appendix, but in summary here's what he's dealing with:

Personal debt	€290,653
Investment property debt	€610,000
Business debt	€20,000
Total Debt	**€920,653**

Now, for the hard facts. Jack is in default on a number of loans, including his mortgage. The protection of the family home is of the utmost importance. His income no longer supports his lifestyle, which further increases the pressure. He cannot turn to his company, which is in free fall, with accumulated losses and a reducing turnover in a very difficult economy. Any hope of ever paying off his mortgage is disappearing, so if he doesn't do something it will cost him his home. The banks are unwilling to do anything to facilitate this man to restructure or to aid his recovery. Jack hasn't a clue where to turn or what to do next.

The possible solutions include:

a)   An increase in property values – unlikely this side of 2020.
b)   New working capital from the bank – no hope.
c)   A significant upswing in Jack's turnover – highly un-likely as Jack is paralysed by inaction as he struggles to cope.
d)   Selling land or houses for whatever he can – banks won't agree.
e)   Settling the balance with the bank.

The likelihood is that Jack will probably keep clinging on until the company folds, which will remove his total income, because as a self-employed person he can't claim social welfare – the choice to pay more PRSI and claim social welfare is unavailable to the self-employed.

In cases like this, where I have met with married couples in this situation, the man will always be looking for an option to hang on, or he will try to find something that he feels he is missing that could solve the problem, whereas the woman just wants to put an end to the misery and have her husband back. I'm with the lady on this one. So what *should* Jack do? How can he even start to deal with his four major problems:

a)   Family home threatened due to mortgage in arrears and sliding further.

b)   Personal income declining, creating more overdraft debt.

c)   Difficulty servicing existing debt.

d)   Source of what little income is left edging towards collapse.

It's like being in a sinking boat in the middle of the ocean. It's sinking because it's carrying too much. Wouldn't you dump everything to keep the boat afloat, irrespective of the consequences? Here's what I'd do without giving it a second thought:

1.   Place all assets other than the family home on the market. At this point, don't even tell the bank. They are not relevant unless there are firm offers on the table. Then approach the bank. More on this in Chapter Seven.

2.   Take all rental income from the investment properties and give twenty-five per cent of it to the bank, keeping the other seventy-five per cent back to service the home loan and get out of arrears. Once again, do this without asking for permission and ignore the strongly worded letters that will come from the banks.

3.   Write to the bank and advise them that you intend to meet them to discuss an exit strategy from your current arrangements. Tell them that there is an action plan and when you are better informed you will present an application for debt resolution.

4.   Use the maximum approved overdraft in the company to open a new bank account for a newly formed company. Go back to the old bank and capitalise the overdraft over ten years.

5. Prepare a statement of affairs for the company with a view to winding it down. See Appendix.

6. Prepare a business plan for a new business as though you were starting out, but with the benefit of the experience and learning you have gained. Ensure that the new company dumps any dead wood or inherited costs.

7. Decide which staff you would re-hire and how much you would pay them this time. Decide which clients are worth keeping. Decide how you can make NewCo better than OldCo – how you will attract new business and understand what is required of you to have a shot at a second chance. Decide that you will have strict disciplines in NewCo and that there will be no baggage of any kind from OldCo.

8. Advise your landlord that you need to terminate your lease as your company is going to cease trading.

9. Advise all staff of the date of cessation. Advise them that you cannot pay redundancy and how to claim their statutory redundancy from the Department of Social Protection.

10. Assuming you can't meet your liabilities to creditors, call a creditors' meeting for a Friday evening, somewhere that it will take an effort to get to. At that meeting set out your statement of affairs, tell your creditors that you cannot afford your own liquidation and call on any non-secured creditors to fund it. You will (likely) find no volunteers but you will have met your responsibility as a director.

One week later, I would suggest doing the following:

1. Offer your landlord a new deal at today's market rent for the property you occupied; they are unlikely to rent it to anyone else in the short term.

2. Recruit new staff. Try calling in the best of your old staff first. They're still entitled to their redundancy from OldCo but you can set a new salary in NewCo.

3. Your new bank account is set up and in credit. No more facility fees or charges for bounced cheques. No crazy interest payments.

4. Go back to your best customers and win them back by convincing them that you can now give them the one-to-one service that they need and used to get before OldCo got into trouble.

5. Use cash instead of credit and pay as you go where possible so that you avoid running up creditors' lists again. Suggest the same when it comes to debtors.

6. Remind yourself daily – no baggage from the old company. No interference from pissed off creditors. That is why you called a creditors' meeting. They had their chance to take action.

Some might say that these action points are unscrupulous, unfair or corrupt. I would say that those people have never looked into the eyes of their children knowing that they didn't have next week's grocery money, never mind a mortgage payment. A desperate man or woman will do whatever they need to do to provide for their children. To anyone who might say that this course of action could destroy the fabric of the economy I say, if we don't start again we will destroy the fabric of the economy anyway. It was the SMEs, self-employed entrepreneurs, who built the Irish economy over the last fifty years. Farmers, builders, car salesmen, grocers, florists, jewellers and so on, who provided employment and vision, moved this country forward, not bankers, not politicians, not the dark suits and certainly not the establishment. Without that entrepreneurial spirit, Ireland, and especially the next generation, is utterly banjaxed. Make no mistake about it, the multinationals will eventually pack up and move away if we lose our corporation tax advantage, which is a real possibility under future EU fiscal agreements (why would the EU agree to give one country an advantage over another if we are all supposed to share fiscal compliance?), or because Ireland becomes fundamentally too risky a jurisdiction for them to do business in – perhaps because we didn't do enough to protect indigenous business. Ireland needs local business along with foreign investment, but the balance at this point is completely one-sided.

The action plan listed above will only work for someone like Jack if he follows through on the business side and then deals with his personal debt by negotiating a satisfactory resolution with the bank. Assuming that he has a successful negotiation which allows him to keep his family home (details in Chapter Seven), Jack will find himself starting all over again with a new business. Granted, a much smaller operation, but at least he will have protected his family home. Given his age profile, he also has the opportunity to build the business again while simultaneously planning for retirement and maybe a third-level education for his kids, as opposed to struggling for the rest of his life and at best continuing to service interest-only repayments on his mortgage, later facing retirement with a large share of his mortgage still owing.

The Irish people were entitled to a transparent and regulated banking system. In the event that we did not receive such a system, we were entitled to strong leadership which would ensure those responsible for the corruption in the system that brought the country to its knees would be brought to justice. I think it's fair to say that we got neither. I had no government, economy, Central Bank or European partners to bail me out when the rug was pulled from under me in business. My acceptance of the established system of governance and banking in Ireland ended on the day the Irish government treated me with contempt by telling me Ireland would not seek a bailout. We live in a society where the Minister for Finance has publicly said that 'we can't believe the banks; we can't believe what they say'.[16] Unbelievable. In four years we've gone from the late Brian Lenihan telling us in the emergency budget of April 2009 that we had turned a corner as a country,[17] to the fiasco of the terms of our bank bailout eighteen months later, to the shambolic performance as a leader from Brian Cowen, to the meek Enda Kenny who claimed that Ireland had achieved a seismic improvement to its national debt negotiation with Europe at the EU summit in June 2012, when the reality was that it was the Italian president Mario Monti who stood up to lead at that now infamous summit, allowing Ireland to jump on his coat tails.[18]

Ireland had lost credibility in my view and for that reason I

---

16   http://www.irishexaminer.com/ireland/kfsnsnidqlid/rss2/

17   http://www.independent.ie/national-news/wikileaks/top-diplomat-be-mused-by-turned-the-corner-speech-2664949.html

18   http://www.businessweek.com/articles/2012-06-29/what-really-hap-pened-at-the-european-summit

decided to do whatever I needed to do to start again, to become an active participant in my own rescue because there was no one else to do it. I invoked my own Chapter 11. I decided to give myself a second chance. I would stay on the right side of the law but I would be unscrupulous if necessary and I would not struggle with guilt. I had failed in many things, but I also felt that I had been failed by a system in which I had trusted, yet which was not going to help me pick up the pieces.

Everyone should have a Plan B. Ireland needs fighting spirit. It needs people to develop and create and employ. Think positively about moving forward and forget about any failings of the past. It's beautifully summed up with the proverb 'Don't look where you fell, look where you slipped'. Look carefully at your life and not just life today. Realise that there are certain targets that we should endeavour to achieve, such as having our mortgage cleared before we retire, ensuring we can cover third-level education costs for our children and that we will have an income in retirement. People are facing into their mid-fifties with massive mortgages remaining. What's the plan for paying a fifteen-year mortgage when you're fifty-five and due to retire in ten years? What about your pension? These were the things that bothered me. It wasn't just the here and now, but the long term. I am forty-four writing this and I want to be able to create a pension for myself and see my life's work result in having some way to give my kids a start in life. I want a rainy-day fund and I certainly want to have my mortgage sorted by the time I am due to retire. We must all plan and think of the longer-term future as well as our survival in the here and now. So many Irish people are surviving from week to week with no plan for the future. For me that's as much living on the edge as Jack's situation. If you are struggling as much now or worse than you were in 2009, then you have not progressed or reacted enough. Identify the obstacles that remain between you and some quality of life both now and in the future, and decide how to act to remove them.

To summarise:

- Create a very detailed statement of affairs.
- Complete management accounts of your company.
- Redesign your statement of affairs assuming that your company were to cease trading. Examine the effect on your financial position.
- Decide if you need to liquidate or just cease trading.
- Prepare a Plan B.
- Prepare to do a deal on all property with your bank (more details in Chapter Seven).
- Give yourself a second chance.

This quote from Johann Wolfgang von Goethe sums it up for me:

I have come to the frightening conclusion that I am the decisive element. It is my personal approach that creates the climate. It is my daily mood that makes the weather. I possess tremendous power to make life miserable or joyous. I can be a tool of torture or an instrument of inspiration; I can humiliate or humour, hurt or heal. In all situations, it is my response that decides whether a crisis is escalated or de-escalated, and a person humanised or de-humanised. If we treat people as they are, we make them worse. If we treat people as they ought to be, we help them become what they are capable of becoming.

It's our response that decides whether a crisis is escalated or de-escalated. How have you responded?

Key Lesson: Only you can end the financial crisis that you find yourself in. Only you can rescue your business and only you can create a better quality of life for yourself, but you must decide what you're prepared to do. Don't wait. Don't assume or hope for change. Demand it and create it. Take your second chance. It's now or never.

6

Good banks, bad banks, ugly banks

It's through cooperation, rather than conflict, that your greatest successes will be derived.

Ralph Charell

Vince Cable, Britain's Business Secretary, told a joke at a business lunch in London in January 2011:[19]

What's the difference between a dead cat on the motorway and a dead banker on the motorway?
There are skid marks around the dead cat.

It sums up the feelings of a generation these days. While researching this chapter I discovered in an article on the Central Bank's website that, in many or all instances, banks apply the following criteria when assessing their potential customers for loans:[20]

---

19 http://www.guardian.co.uk/theguardian/2011/jan/30/jokes-about-bankers
20 http://www.centralbank.ie/mpolbo/assetman/Pages/riskmanagement.aspx

- Currency risk
- Credit risk
- Market risk
- Liquidity risk
- Operational risk

The article refers to banks facing these risks in their efforts to conduct business. It seems to me, however, that this has been turned on its head and that these headings now describe the risk for individuals of doing business with a bank. Despite all that has happened, both domestically and globally, we continue to see blatant disrespect from banks all over the world for the many millions of people that bailed them out. Between May and July of 2012 alone, we saw the Libor scandal that engulfed banks in the UK,[21] the disastrous actions of JP Morgan trader Bruno Iksil,[22] the IT disaster that disrupted the business of over 100,000 Ulster Bank/Nat West customers,[23] followed by a banker from Georgia in the United States who disappeared along with $17 million,[24] as well as confirmation that HSBC failed to prevent its services being used to launder Mexican drug money.[25] And all post-bailout, when people are supposed to be able to trust that

---

21   http://www.bbc.co.uk/news/business-18671255

22   http://www.independent.co.uk/news/business/news/the-city-trader-who-lost-2bn-and-he-was-the-risk-expert-who-was-meant-to-play-it-safe-7738004.html

23   http://www.bbc.co.uk/news/business-18575932

24   http://www.cbsnews.com/8301-201_162-57470035/missing-banker-aubrey-lee-price-confesses-he-lost-$17m-of-investors-money-in-purported-suicide-note/

25   http://www.bbc.co.uk/news/business-18880269

the banks have been reprimanded and are far more tightly controlled.

It would be naive to think that such losses don't cost each of us in some form, even if they are not happening on home turf. These episodes make all the other banks nervous and create reasons to increase accruals against losses and embezzlement, which all filters down to increasing fees for the general customer. Once upon a time being a banker in Ireland, or anywhere, carried a certain cachet and respect, but times have changed and now banker is almost a dirty word. High-profile names in Irish banking have been shamed into retirement, facing hostile press, finance committee probes, and pending possible legal proceedings from both the Director of Public Prosecutions and the Office of the Director of Corporate Enforcement, but behind the very public faces of the Irish banking collapse, there are teams of people who have also played a role in the story. I would characterise them as follows:

1. Individuals on a power trip/bullies: those who caused horrendous strain and anxiety with the shameful and disrespectful approach they took to dealing with people struggling to cope in the face of a crisis that the very bank recklessly pursuing them was partially to blame for! I have experienced this first-hand.

2. Clueless individuals/incompetents: those who were in-adequately trained to understand the gravity of the situation for a customer when difficulties occurred. Their inability to act in a commercial and rational manner resulted in further distress to many people. I have also experienced this first-hand.

3. Traumatised individuals: those who suffered emotionally themselves, having been placed in situations where they were both aware of and empathetic to their customers' needs, but not equipped or supported to deal with depressed and in some cases suicidal customers. Bank officials with whom I have been dealing communicated this problem to me after *Shepherd's Pie* was published.

4. Insightful and pragmatic individuals: those who could see that the banks were on the wrong road. Those who could see the humanitarian damage that they were causing. Those who wanted to learn from past mistakes and heal the pain their organisation had caused. Those bankers who wanted everyone, both the bank and the customer, to be able to move on. I have also experienced this first-hand.

My journey since 2008 has exposed me to good banks, bad banks and very ugly banks, and I have learned how to cope with all three in a way that works for me and that I hope will work for others – that's my primary motivator for writing this book.

I believe that it is critical to be proactive in creating our own recovery to survive in business. That would be my number one piece of advice for any businessperson trying to cope. But I also believe that the second most important thing is to educate people on how to communicate with post-bailout banks. Irish people tend to still deal with banks like we did ten years ago, when it was easy to borrow and we still had respect for bankers, trusted them and thought we had a personal relationship with them. It is no longer realistic to expect your local bank manager to sanction a loan based on a nod or a phone call. Branch managers have very little power now. They are at the bottom of the managerial food chain. As in any business that suddenly loses a huge amount of money, bank procedures changed radically, even before the new layers of regulation became an unfortunate reality, yet customers didn't seem to get it. Customers didn't buy into the change and the reasons behind it, and blamed the change in their access to funds from banks on the 'lack of credit'.

However, after 2011 the lack of credit for many people resulted from a lack of knowledge, a lack of transparency, a lack of communication, a lack of preparation and, ultimately, a lack of strategy. This doesn't forgive the appalling lack of courtesy and respect afforded to many decent people all over this country, but I think it's fair to say that many of them were not equipped for the new procedures at the banks because they had grown accustomed to an informal and easygoing relationship with their friendly bank manager. When the crisis hit, heads were buried in the sand and not too many people chose to engage with their lenders. Some went looking for fresh working capital for companies that were either insolvent or had the potential to be, without a business plan. There was a lot of panic and ignorance because people had never had to deal with this altered banking system before. So, when customers who were in for millions with their banks wanted to broach the issue of debt forgiveness in the hope that they could start over or try to recover in any way, this ignorance did a lot of damage.

There are two sides to the story of the relationship between Irish borrowers and Irish banks. I hope that I can convey both sides accurately and that doing so might help to change the relationship so that it works for both. There is no doubt, I was one of the most ignorant when it came to trying to deal with banks. Seán and Tommy at ACT, however, were not. They were interacting with banks on a daily basis. When I was a kid, I used to play a game with my friends where we'd tie a piece of string between two cans, run in two different directions taking a can each and then I would hold my can to my ear while my friend spoke into the other one. Tommy and Seán were the piece of string between the cans for me with the banks. I will be forever grateful to them for teaching me how to face the challenge of dealing with a lender to whom I was indebted.

The tipping point in my relationship with the banks came one day as I walked through Gladstone Street in Clonmel. A senior official from Bank A in Cork called me on my mobile. I didn't have a good relationship with him. I felt that he was stiff, lacking any empathy. I was fatigued and totally stressed out. It was early 2010. The call ended with me shouting and swearing at him, furious with his request and with his attitude. Two days later Tommy came to see me and tore strips off me for the way I had behaved towards the official. He explained that the banker was my 'agent on the inside'. Convince him, impress him and he would sell my credibility within the bank, three levels higher. Piss him off and pitching the idea of George Mordaunt Inc. as a viable option for recovery would be over before it even started. Tommy quickly arranged a meeting in Cork to clear the air. Within ten days of the blowout on the phone, the bank official and I were sitting across from each other. Tommy explained that it was a difficult situation for all of us and that nothing would be achieved unless we both understood the task at hand and respected each other's position and opinion. At that meeting, the bank official I had spoken to on the phone, and another who was attending the meeting, helped me to understand how the bank viewed the position of borrowers who were struggling. I helped them to understand that no matter what I tried to do, my debt was so huge I would never be able to clear it all, but that I wanted to face the issue head on and do whatever I could, and I was not trying to hide.

In that meeting, I sat before the banker who I had treated with contempt (and vice versa) ten days earlier, talking honestly to him and admitting I was broke but not hiding or avoiding, and asking, 'Now what do we do?' I was surprised by the response. It wasn't 'Get the hell out of my office and find our money', but instead, 'We don't know. The bank hasn't got that far yet.' It was a fantastic answer because it was genuine and credible. The bank simply hadn't got that far. They (and plenty of others) hadn't figured out a road map to dealing with the hard-core debt in Irish business and society without causing havoc. That bank official went on to explain to me the difference between debt forgiveness and debt write-off. It was the first time I had heard of such a difference, but it was quite distinct. He explained that in a debt forgiveness situation, the bank would acknowledge the genuine and transparent efforts of the borrower to address and resolve their debt burden while recognising that the borrower might never be able to fully repay, and so would work with them towards a mutually acceptable solution. The borrower could, thereby, be left in their home and with some kind of acceptable lifestyle. But in a debt write-off situation, the bank believes that the borrower is hiding assets or trying it on just to get out of paying off the debt, without fully and transparently showing all of their hand. In this case the bank will go after the borrower for everything they've got, including the family home, furniture, car and jewellery, right down to their wedding ring. What he seemed to be saying, and this is purely my own interpretation of it, is:

a)   We don't have a process but we're working on one.
b)   We will reward those who work with us.
c)   We will penalise those who don't/won't.

By the time the meeting ended, I felt that I had been educated. I was no longer ignorant and, in the process, had mended a relationship with my 'inside agent'. At that meeting I had agreed to go home and prepare a very detailed suite of information about George Mordaunt Inc., with the sole objective of creating a strategy for dealing with my business and personal debt. After two-and-a-half years of angst, it was the first sign that my situation with a bank might change for the better. I hasten to add that I wasn't experiencing the same appetite for change from other banks. It seemed that this one was starting to think differently to the others. Some of my meetings with another bank were a disaster. They seemed to be the ones with their heads buried in the sand when it came to dealing with reality. I know now that they themselves were in deep trouble about which I had no idea at the time, and for all the pressure they had heaped on me and all the things that they criticised me for trying in business, they had effectively run out of steam too. They hadn't yet received a bailout, but they were headed towards full nationalisation.

My plan now was to take one step at a time, put one foot in front of the other and deal with each bank as best I could

– which I think was a mirror image of what the bank in Cork was doing with their distressed customers. These were uncharted waters for both borrowers and bankers, and we were all trying to find our way. The issue of debt reduction in any form was, and is, very sensitive. I may have been a test case. I continued to meet with that bank official throughout the year. I let him know that I was writing a book about coping with the recession and that I would be sharing the experience I had had with some banks. I was quite worried about what his reaction to that might be but he seemed to be largely disinterested – so long as he had been informed, I felt I had done my bit.

By the spring of 2011 the press were very focused on debt forgiveness for mortgage holders in very high negative equity. Media attention was keeping the pressure on banks to lend and to address the debt problem or write down loans. On the face of it, nothing was really happening but, as the year went on, I found myself at meetings with officials at higher levels of banking both because of the extent of my borrowings and because of the relationships ACT had with the bank officials, who would talk very openly in their presence. I felt that progress was being made on the taboo subject of debt forgiveness, albeit slow or even invisible – but I sensed that some kind of movement wasn't far away.

Then the first breakthrough came. On 4 April 2011, David Hodgkinson, the executive chairman of AIB, said that they were considering many different options to deal with their problem cases, including debt forgiveness.[26] This announce-

---

26   http://www.irishtimes.com/newspaper/breaking/2011/0413/breaking4.html

ment came on the back of the bank posting a loss of €10.4 billion for 2010. While this certainly boded well, it was still focused on home-mortgage arrears, which I felt was putting the cart before the horse. There wasn't very much discussion happening around debt forgiveness for self-employed people who had grafted for two decades and were facing catastrophic losses on commercial property, which would hold them, and their ability to employ, back. Every employed Irish worker has made an individual contribution to the success of the Irish economy since the foundation of the State, whether employed in a multinational, an SME or self-employed, in the public or private sector; however, in my view, Ireland Inc. was built on the back of hard labour from self-employed entrepreneurs, from farmers to builders to corner-shop owners, and we need to encourage and support those people to help create our future economy too. Multinationals certainly contribute to local economies, but inevitably they repatriate large portions of their profits and have no hesitation moving their operations if the circumstances that favour their business in a country change. Hence I believe that our government needs to recognise and address the plight of indigenous Irish business as much if not more than the problem of mortgage debt.

I continued meeting with Bank A and in the summer of 2011 they accepted that I should put up for sale any and all commercial and residential investment properties I had, and come back to them with any firm offers I might receive, after which we could discuss any potential (likely) residual debt and decide whether I could proceed to sell. I kept my mind focused on my ultimate goal and set about disposing of each property. It wasn't an easy task.

By the time my next reviews with all the banks with which I had loans came around, it was late 2011 and my book had been published and was getting a lot of media attention. I didn't know it, but one bank was carefully monitoring everything I was saying and doing. About a week before I returned to meet with the bank in Cork, I was told by the bank official that his boss would like to meet me, having read the book, so they would be sitting in on the meeting. My heart sank and I thought, Christ, I've pissed somebody right off. In a recent interview I had called for bank officials to be trained in some kind of mental health safety before any of them were left in a room with a distressed creditor. By then I had heard or read the terrible stories of hundreds of small business owners being bullied by bank officials. Grown adults were being utterly traumatised by bankers. Many had been struggling for almost three years to just survive, never mind being able to pay anything to their banks. They were fragile and the slightest threat could push them over the edge. Yet they had been threatened and intimidated behind closed doors. The increase in suicides as a result of financial pressure had been heavily covered in the press. Of all the letters I received and stories I heard, one of the most disturbing is about the effect an individual bank official had. I have changed some of the circumstances to protect the identity of the individual involved.

Kevin was sixty-one and married with adult kids. He was the joint owner of a hugely successful hotel group. He and his business partner had borrowed over €40 million for the development of their business interests and land. They were servicing all of this debt with the exception of a €2 million loan, which he didn't explain. They were tax compliant and employed over forty people. They had always paid their way but this €2 million loan was difficult for many reasons and as a result it landed them in front of a senior bank official at an Irish bank. For months this official had picked away at Kevin. He had pushed and pressured and threatened to the point where Kevin was struggling emotionally. After a very heated exchange at a meeting, Kevin decided that he could not go to work the next day. He was terrified and distraught because the banker was threatening to seek a winding up order against the business, despite its strong performance. It was a clear case of a banker using his authority irresponsibly rather than productively, and recognising that this business was still viable.

No longer able to cope and not able to motivate himself to dress for work, Kevin sat down and wrote himself a letter, which he later shared with me when I met him after my story was published. I was blown away. How brave he was, talking about how he felt so candidly and sharing such a personal letter with me. When we met we spoke for two hours and I gave him all the information I could based on my own experiences, and I put him in touch with ACT. To my great surprise that evening I received an email from Kevin, with the letter attached, giving his permission to bring it into the public domain in the hope that it might help someone else, or effect some change:

Hello to all involved in business and negotiations.

I am not in the office today. I am working from home and not having a good day. I didn't sleep much last night and many other nights, I am suffering severe headaches for the last couple of months, my head is spinning and I need you to know my thoughts. If they are all over the place please forgive me.

This person

I haven't enjoyed one day of my life since I met this person (a bank official). What a bad feeling and cloud to live under at 61 years of age.

Primary school

The last time I got this feeling was in primary school, where I was beaten on a daily basis by an abusive 'Christian' brother. I was lashed with his crooked cane on the hands and legs for his own perverted reasons. I hated life so much back then that I cried every morning of my school life and only got happiness during summer and other breaks and eventually when I left school at the age of 13.

Fifty years on

I now don't like going to work like I didn't like going to school all those years ago. I made myself a promise that I would never again live under that pressure but I am back to that feeling and it says a lot for the abuse and bullying I am enduring today. I am being mistreated, bullied, suffering an abuse of power by this bank official in his role as a bank employee.

Life in between

I am not one to complain as can be seen from my short story. At age 20 my grandfather, father, mother, grandmother and uncle all died within a 14-month period, as well as my best friend, and I was involved in the accident which killed my friend. I was sad, very sad but got on with life as I had a ready-made family to take care of. These happenings were the will of God so I could handle this, but the will of the bank official in action is killing me.

Family

I had five younger siblings to rear with the help of my young girlfriend, now my wife. We managed, grew up together (seven of us) without any state help, without any financial help from any quarter, without any social services help. Except for the goodness of my mother's sisters and my good remaining uncle, we were alone in the world.

Business

I have been successfully self-employed all of my life and have employed hundreds of people during that time, paid millions in taxes to the exchequer and am tax compliant in all my dealings now and always, every supplier and landlord has always been paid on time and in full for over 40 years, I do not have one bad debt now or ever, I have always paid my bank repayments in full and on time, even through these difficult times I have met interest and some capital repayments on all but one loan.

Where I am now

Where I find myself now, is worse than anything I have experienced in my life so far. The abuse of power and disrespect shown to me during this crisis is almost intolerable. These one-sided negotiations with the bank in their favour make me feel like a criminal or fraudster. I am not taking this any more. I am looking for a fairer hearing, a fairer deal, a two-sided negotiation to work out our problems. I feel that the banks got a fair deal recently when NAMA gave them a lifeline and kept them alive; it would also be a fair deal if we got a lifeline instead of the pressure that is being applied.

I want to go to Phil Hogan to take our case to Enda Kenny to try to show what is happening to our viable business at the hands of an unfair bank employee, who is steering us into a default situation instead of a rescue package.

I will not be able to sign these documents [letters of sanction/additional security/or relating to higher interest charges] without the addition of something like:

Signed under duress
Signed under threat of receivership
Signed with a gun to my head
Signing out of a sense of duty to my business partner

It's powerful. Kevin wanted the letter to be read to Enda Kenny. I'm not sure it has made it that far, but I managed to read it, with his permission, on national radio. I spoke about it in the media and maybe, this time, it will make it into the hands of the Taoiseach. I wonder whether, when he sat down to write it, he really thought it would ever make a difference to anyone. It certainly had a huge impact on me. I see Kevin as another person who has answered the question 'what are you prepared to do' and shows true grit as far as I'm concerned.

Kevin's story was one of many that I received where the common theme was that people were terrified of bankers. It was clear to me, based on this and on my own experiences, that certain bank officials were on some kind of power trip. I was motivated and invigorated by people like Kevin and my soft-spoken friend who called me having climbed down off the paint cans. I had an opportunity to push back with the banks. I had access to the media. I could say what they couldn't say, so I did. There have been consequences, like the registered letter that was delivered during Christmas week 2011 seeking a repayment of over €500,000 from liquidated companies for which one bank held personal guarantees. The bank is not stupid – they knew they could retrieve no money, but the message was clear to me: 'Shut your mouth or else.' It was the same week that I had appeared on the RTÉ evening news telling people to stand up to banks.

That was the ugly side of banking, but I was also about to experience the proactive side. Like I said, I thought I'd really pissed someone off with all I had been saying in the media about banking bullies, so I was not expecting my meeting to be a particularly pleasant one. However, much to my surprise the bank's representative didn't want to talk about my debt or my business difficulties. Instead we spoke about the trauma in both trenches. They told me of suicides among bank staff, the mental health issues suffered by staff who had been given instructions to carry out impossible tasks without training or support, who had no idea how to tackle the loan books and were miserable about the part they were being forced to play in their customers' trauma. It was happening all over the country and, having experienced it myself on the customer side, I can only imagine how difficult it must have been for untrained bank officials to cope with that pressure. They also told me how stress levels among bank staff were reaching critical point and the HR department was looking to address the problem not only for bank customers, but also for its own staff.

The bank's representative also acknowledged that many officials had disgraced themselves and their employers with their lack of compassion. They had recently attended a meeting where a colleague verbally brutalised a man of seventy-two years of age for failing to meet his obligations. They interrupted and asked the man how long he had been a customer of that bank. He said fifty-two years and, with that, he broke down. At that point they unilaterally decided that this hardline approach would cease with immediate effect and that they would work with this man to bring about a resolution that was acceptable to both parties. The bank's representative went on to explain to me that a decision had been made at the highest level to rebuild the bank, recognising that if it were to exist in fifty years time it would need my children and their children to open their accounts with them. The bank accepted that mistakes had been made on both sides of the borrowing and lending relationship and that a different approach would be required for both sides to move forward. The approach would be respectful and one that proactively addressed customers' debt burden.

It was a few weeks after this meeting that this bank organised a courier to collect copies of *Shepherd's Pie* from me in Clonmel. My story was to assist in educating bank officials about what it was like to be a distressed borrower dealing with a bank. It was a proud moment for me, knowing that something good might have come from my trauma, but when they asked if I would be willing to work with them to help spread the message that they were changing the way they dealt with people in trouble, I felt honoured. I still owed them millions, but I was witnessing a seismic shift in the banking sector. It was a turning point for the bank and its customers and the beginning of a new era. I hope that one day there will be portraits of this official and their colleagues who have instigated this new approach on the walls of the bank's headquarters, as the founders of the new model of banking in Ireland.

Inspired by this banker and motivated by the people still contacting me to seek advice, I wrote to the chief executive officer of another bank with whom I had debt (let's call it Bank B) and whose approach was not quite as cooperative. I explained that many of his customers were contacting me and that their stories were similar, claiming they had not been treated with any kind of respect by the bank officials with whom they were dealing, although I hadn't had the same difficulties with that bank myself. The CEO's response was:

Dear Mr Mordaunt

Thank you for sending me a copy of your book.

I note your comments regarding contacts you have received from [this Bank's] customers. The consistent advice we offer to all of our customers is to come and talk to us as soon as they believe they have an issue. We are fully committed to working with customers who are prepared to work with us in finding an acceptable and workable solution for the customer and the Bank.

We have and continue to put a great deal of effort into training and developing our people and in designing workable solutions for personal and business customers and our experience to date is that this approach is enabling us to support our customers through this very difficult time.

I would suggest that you advise any customer who has made contact with you in this regard to contact their local branch or their relevant relationship manager. They will find people in our branches who are willing and able to work with them and help them through the challenges they face.

Thank you again for your book and best wishes with your business.

Meanwhile, despite all I had learned about engaging with banks, it takes two to tango and I was still having heated exchanges with Bank C. They were impossible. I often left meetings with them feeling like a fool. I would explain the progress I was making and they would laugh, as if I were making it up. I argued week in and week out about their fluctuating cost of funding and how it was making it impossible for me to keep up. Their interest charges just kept climbing and climbing. I owed them €2.8 million. I became so stressed out by their actions that I sought advice on the escalating interest costs from a highly respected, independent financial advisor with whom ACT and I then worked. The increased charges were referred to in the loan sanction letter as 'embedded cost of funds'.[27] What did that mean? Nobody could explain it to me. The embedded cost of funds was climbing so high that the extra burden was threatening the actual business – a quarterly payment of €9000 on a loan of €2.8 million had risen to a quarterly payment of €17,000. I was servicing the €9,000,

---

27 These were fixed costs with other lenders, so I hadn't come across this as an issue previously.

and even when the repayment went to €17,000, I made the payments, but it kept increasing, which continued to worsen my trading position and created higher losses. The higher the losses, the worse my credit profile became and so it went on in a circle. I needed help urgently to stem this particular flow of loss and communicate clearly to the bank how the fluctuating cost of funds was having a detrimental effect on my business. The financial advisor put it far more succinctly than I:

Dear George

We refer to our recent discussion and your request for us to review the interest rates currently being charged on facilities provided by [Bank C] to both Brian Mordaunt & Sons Ltd and you personally with Brian Mordaunt Senior and Brian Mordaunt Junior. In this regard we can comment as follows:

On both facilities, the rate of interest applied can be broken down into three separate elements:

1. 3 Month Euribor Rate
2. Margin and
3. Embedded Funding Cost

The 3 Month Euribor Rate is largely outside of the bank's control and is the rate set by the European Central Bank (ECB) on funds lent to independent Financial Institutions. The rate applied of 1.266% is consistent with what you would be charged by other financial institutions.

The Margin is the profit element set by the bank on the facilities provided and is at the bank's discretion how much they wish to charge. The interest rates charged of 2% and 3% on these facilities would not be outside the normal commercial lending terms of any Irish Financial Institution in the current climate.

It is the third and final element of the interest charge which is causing the significant increase in interest rates applied to the facilities outlined. The Embedded Funding Cost is by definition a sunk cost, directly related to the internal costs of the Financial Institution, in this case [Bank C]. It is derived from a complex formula incorporating the interest expense of the Financial Institution over set revenue thresholds as a fraction of the average total debt of the Financial Institution for the most recent two years. In [Bank C's] instance, on the two facilities provided, this interest rate has risen 288% since 2009 (from 1.1039% to 3.508%) on the Brian Mordaunt & Sons Ltd facility and an astounding 965% since 2009 (from .3295% to 3.508%) on your personal facilities.

The marketplace at the moment is offering commercial lending rates of circa 4.8%, a far cry from the combined rates offered above of 7.774% and 6.774%. In our experience, no other Financial Institution is incorporating such extortionate costs into their interest rates. Clearly, you are being asked to absorb [Bank C's] own precarious gearing position arising from its exposure to current fluctuations for similar products on the market and a lack of prudence in matching (at the time of the advance) its own funding position with that of the products that were being sold to its customers. This mismatch was 'plugged' by the Embedded Funding Cost element, the implications of which we are certain you were not aware of at the time.

Your business has already been seriously impacted by the downturn in the economy and as such is in survival mode. If the business has to pay such crippling interest rates, it is highly likely that this will eventually lead to the complete erosion of your cash-flow position and ultimately the closure of the business.

It is hardly credible to believe that you understood the impact of the arrangement you entered into and accordingly we believe you would have a good case to bring before the Financial Ombudsman.

We would hope this adequately satisfies your enquiry, but should you wish to discuss this further, please do not hesitate to contact us.

This confirmed that between January 2010 and April 2011 the cost of interest on that loan had climbed by 965 per cent. No matter what I did, no matter how I tried to engage with that bank to point this out and reason with them, they ignored all my efforts. They absolutely refused to engage – they rejected the concept of an exit strategy or any of the possibilities I was discussing with Bank A. In the absence of leadership from the State, I passed this letter to the bank, but their response was dismissive and I got nowhere. These two banks both reported to the Department of Finance, were both owned by the Irish people, yet their strategies could not have been more different and clearly there was no State control or State-defined strategy that nationalised banks had to follow. I believe that Bank C's strategy is stalling the recovery of small businesses and, in turn, the general economy – and as its owner, the State should make a call on this practice.

The subject of the cost of borrowing from this bank was debated in Dáil Éireann in the spring of 2012, but by then the damage was done. The bank had charged customers close to seven per cent interest on any kind of loan other than fixed- or tracker-rate mortgages, by passing on the 'embedded cost of funds'. These variable funding costs were applied by other lenders. Bank C had effectively levied burdensome interest charges on mortgage customers with variable rates to try to plug the gaps caused not only by their losses on tracker mortgages but by their borrowing for the short term while lending money long term. When most banks borrow on the open market, they do so on a long-term basis. So if you borrow say €200,000 for a mortgage, the bank will normally borrow the money to fund that over a three- or five-year period. However, Irish banks made a fundamental error of judgement in their exposure, as they slowly became locked out of the bond market and could only access fresh borrowings if they paid significantly higher interest rates. Bank C had clearly decided that their customers should pay for their error. This is why their wording in sanction letters contained the woolly term 'embedded cost of funds' and this, along with their exposure to tracker mortgages, explains why they charged such extraordinarily high interest rates. The irony of course is that the bank only survived because it was bailed out at the expense of the people. By the time Bank C was fully re-capitalised by the Irish taxpayer, Irish people had spent almost €70 billion bailing out the Irish banking system.[28] That figure

---

28 http://namawinelake.wordpress.com/2012/06/11/2011-annual-reports-for-irish-banks-reveal-potentially-catastrophic-losses-and-additional-bail-outs-requirements/

represented forty-five per cent of our total GDP in 2011. €34.7 billion was injected into Anglo alone.

In June 2012 the executive chairman of Bank C wrote to every customer to apologise for the behaviour of the bank up to that point. Specific reference was made to their abnormally high interest charges.

Dear George,

I was recently appointed as Chief Executive of [Bank C]. I wanted to take an early opportunity to communicate with you directly to share my views on the bank and on some important commitments and decisions which we have taken.

However, to start with, I want to make it very clear that I don't believe that [the bank] has performed to an acceptable standard in recent years. As a result of some of the bank's decisions and actions, the Irish taxpayer has had to invest substantial funds when those funds could have been used much better elsewhere. Many of the bank's customers have suffered financially because of the impact of decisions which should not have been taken. I apologise for the mistakes which were made and I am determined to do all in my power to rectify them.

We have now commenced on a journey to do just that. That journey will take time and no doubt there will be frustrations along the way – for our customers and for ourselves. But I believe that we can look forward to the emergence of a new [bank] over the coming years; more focused and more humble for sure, but also one that reconnects with its customers and enjoys their respect and their loyalty.

As we start on this journey, I want to emphasise four key commitments which I am making on behalf of the bank.

1.   We will be competitive with our rates.
We have a Standard Variable Rate (SVR) that is significantly out of line with the rest of the market. From 14th May we are reducing the home loan SVR and Loan to Value (LTV) Variable Rate by 0.5% to 4.690% meaning lower mortgage repayments in almost 74,500 homes nationwide. We will continue to review all of our rates at regular intervals to make them as competitive as possible.

2.   We will work on getting credit back into the market.
We understand that it can be difficult at the moment getting access to personal credit and we are focused on improving our internal credit policies to address this.

3.   We will work constructively to help our customers in arrears.
We understand that being in arrears is stressful. We have a wide range of options available to help everyone in this situation and we are committed to working constructively on this agenda.

4.   We will act responsibly to protect the investment which the taxpayer has made in the bank.
We are very conscious of the significant investment which the taxpayer has made to support [the] bank at this time. With that in mind we will act responsibly to protect that investment and the value which is in the business.

Finally, we will be open and honest with you. We will endeavour to communicate with you openly and keep you informed. We are committed to doing all we can to rebuild your trust and to repay the loyalty you have shown us in the past few years.

Yours sincerely

I found this letter of apology worthless, particularly given the debris that this bank has left behind. Not only did it contribute to the collapse of the Irish economy, but its subsequent behaviour compounded the problem for hundreds of thousands of people, driving them into arrears on their home loans through the outrageous interest they charged. To my knowledge, they have offered nothing by way of concession to those people who funded them for the damage they did.

***

Four years on from that infamous night in September 2008, not much has changed other than that the people now own two of the original 'big four' banks, with the third in wind down and the fourth moving towards recovery slowly.[29] All four banks continue to lose money and all of them continue, in some form or another, to obstruct economic recovery by not lending, requesting unnecessary receiverships and not publicly setting out their road map for dealing with residential negative

---

29   In September 2008 the Irish government decided to guarantee all deposits and borrowings from the six Irish retail banks for the following two years. The banks covered were Allied Irish Bank, Bank of Ireland, Anglo Irish Bank, Irish Life & Permanent Group, Nationwide Building Society and the Educational Building Society. http://www.rte.ie/news/2008/0930/economy.html

equity and mass commercial failure. Fintan O'Toole wrote in *The Irish Times* that 'Reckless banking wrecks lives.'[30] He noted that 'Ireland has suffered proportionally more damage from reckless banking than any other society.' He and others have called for a financial tax known as a Financial Trading Tax to be introduced on banks. The EU Commission estimates that a 0.1 per cent tax on securities transactions and a 1 per cent tax on derivatives would raise €57 billion annually.[31] It seems like a no-brainer to me, but then it also seems to me that sensible banking decisions have never been to the forefront of our government's agenda. You only have to look at the biggest monster of them all – NAMA – to see that.

My struggles with the Irish banking system continued. I was making headway with Bank A, was in a standoff with Banks B and D and in an ongoing battle with Bank C. But I had learned plenty and at least now I could better understand the workings of these institutions and hence discuss the future more openly. I have nothing to hide from the banks. I have learned that the most important thing you can do when setting out a plan to deal with a bank if you cannot service your debt is to educate yourself. Consider how you present your business plans or any other information they need to have. How should you compile it? How do you know what to ask, who to ask and how to ask for what you need? If your biggest problem is a debt that you simply cannot service, for whatever reason, be it a mortgage or a commercial debt, then

---

30 http://www.irishtimes.com/newspaper/opinion/2012/0710/12243197 20356.html

31 http://www.oxera.com/Oxera/media/Oxera/downloads/reports/The-eco-nomic-impact-of-the-proposed-FTT.pdf?ext=.pdf

read and understand the Consumer Protection Codes on the Central Bank's website. If you are gripped by fear, knowing and understanding what reliefs are available to you will help to remove the fear and get you engaged with the bank.

These are the ten questions that I am most frequently asked about my dealings with banks and my answers:

1   What is the single most important thing that you did to ease the pressure between you and the banks you owe?

I engaged in full-on, open discussions, regularly advising the bank of my intentions clearly and succinctly, without fear, letting them know that I was open to foreclosure as an option as well as assisted disposal of toxic assets in a managed fashion.

2   How did you get them to listen and stop harassing you?

I wrote to them and explained that their behaviour was affecting my mental health and my quality of life and that I had decided it was going to stop. I removed the fear and chose to fight back and treat them with the contempt with which they treated me, and when that didn't work and I was educated in how to engage with them, I reversed the pressure. I constantly wrote, emailed, called and texted. I demonstrated that I was up to creating the solution for as long as they worked with me rather than against me.

3   How do you get on with the bank now?

It ranges from very well to no engagement. Some respect that I am trying to take responsibility by actively selling or leasing to manage my debts, some ignore me because they haven't yet figured out how to solve their own problems, never mind mine, and some are still aggressive – I think that's because I won't shut up about banks and how they should not call all the shots on the issue of debt in this country.

4 Did you get any loans written off?

I am involved in a three-year programme of asset disposal under the guidance of one bank.

5 Is that a yes or a no?

Both. I will still be repaying debt ten years from now, even after any assets have been sold. So that's a yes, but with conditions, in that after I have sold an asset, I will have to repay a proportion of the negative equity that is left after the sale but not necessarily all of it, pending market conditions and my financial status at the time.

6 Where do you see yourself banking in five years time?

AIB without any doubt, because I believe they will exit the current difficulties quicker and with a better understanding of their past mistakes.

7 Will you ever borrow money again?

Instinctively I would say no way, but you can never say never. The bigger question is will anybody ever lend to me again?

8 Do you fear a judgement order?[32]

Absolutely not and that is part of my coping mechanism. I don't expect to exit this period of my life without my credit rating being

---

32   http://www.citizensinformation.ie/en/money_and_tax/personal_finance/debt/enforcement_of_judgments.html

badly damaged. A judgement across a property won't serve any purpose for a bank in the short term in my circumstances because my mortgaged properties are suffering huge negative equity which may never be reversed, so my family home won't sell – therefore it's a futile exercise.

9 Do you feel any guilt about the level of bad debt to banks that you may end up being responsible for, given that now the taxpayer has to pay?

I can rationalise it because my behaviour did not cause the economic collapse of this country and my decisions are not the decisions preventing its recovery. I couldn't control it then and I can't control it now. Property values won't recover because of NAMA and the flooding of the market with fire sale properties, which was a government decision. When I see the highest-ranking bank officials being arrested and facing prosecution I realise that much of this was beyond my control.[33] I made mistakes, but I'm not trying to pull a fast one and I could not have anticipated or legislated for what went on at the highest levels of banking. I accepted the information I had when I made those decisions to borrow for expansion in good faith, and none of that information anticipated the disaster that would befall our economy.

10 Where do you now bank and why?

Ulster Bank, because it was and is the only bank in Clonmel that offers an old-fashioned, relationship-based service. Traditionally,

33 http://www.independent.ie/national-news/courts/fitzpatrick-and-two-former-anglo-executives-sent-for-criminal-trials-3253662.html

banks were built on local knowledge and relationships, and in my opinion the sooner an element of that returns to main-street banking, the better for all of us. If you call your local bank now, you end up talking to a twenty-year-old in a call centre in who knows where. I don't think that's customer service.

I believe that if entrepreneurs had been supported by banks instead of being put out of business and everything handed to civil servants in NAMA, the Irish economy would not still be suffering as much as it is. Surely there was a creative solution to working with property developers and other entrepreneurs rather than removing them from their position at the head of their business where they would have some hope of recovery? The banks were accused of over-lending. I would further accuse them of compounding the issue with their hysterical reaction from 2008. Entrepreneurs achieved great strides of progress in this country and their drive and entrepreneurship created, developed, employed and improved the basic daily services that we have all become used to. To consign so many of them to the scrap heap in a twelve-month period was crazy. If hotel owners, transport companies, developers, restaurant owners and so on had received a reprieve from banks in 2009/2010, they might have traded their way out of trouble, kept people employed and stemmed the collapse of the property market by avoiding going into NAMA or entering receivership.

In most cases that I know of, when a receiver is appointed the trading entity will continue if the receiver secures finance from the bank while charging the same bank for the receiver's fees. The receiver continues to pay the business overhead costs, so why not afford the same freedom to the business owner with conditions such as relinquishing full control over the finances of the business for an agreed period of recovery with regular business reviews, thereby working with the business owner towards recovery but without the exorbitant fees? The drive and determination of commercially minded business people who want their business to survive can't be replaced by the suits at NAMA or accountancy firms. A calm, stepped recovery period, where the combined efforts of the bank and the business owner might lead to a recovered business, rather than a fire sale of the business and the property from which it trades, seems to me to be a more productive approach. There are no winners in the alternative scenario.

In June 2010 an IMF working paper written by Luc Laeven and Fabian Valencia and entitled *Resolution of the Banking Crisis: The Good, the Bad and the Ugly* was published.[34] The subject was the resolution of the banking crisis worldwide. The thirty-six-page report contains a section called 'Banking Crisis Start and End Dates' and lists both a start date and end date for each territory. Beside Ireland it shows the start date as 2008. The end date has been left open, nothing but an ellipsis.

Key Lesson: Educate yourself on how to communicate with banks post-bailout. Prepare thoroughly. Be professional. Identify the problem, present the facts and create the solution. Do so with absolute transparency.

---

34   http://www.imf.org/external/pubs/ft/wp/2010/wp10146.pdf

7

Debt

Forgiveness does not change the past, but it does enlarge the future.

Paul Boese

I referred to debt forgiveness as the national taboo in *Shepherd's Pie*. But it should no longer be taboo and it cannot be ignored as a very real issue and possible way forward for this country. It's also one of the most personal and private elements of my story and is the number one item that I am asked about on a daily basis. I thought long and hard about how I would broach the subject in this book, debating with myself, with my wife, with Seán and Tommy, with my editor. Should I talk about it or not? Long discussions took place in my house every day about how I could tackle it if I decided to include it in the book. Some felt I couldn't go there, others felt it was impossible to tell the full story without some specifics which were quite personal, and my editor agreed with me that it would be a critical chapter. However, my own view was even clearer. My story had been told to this point with nothing left out. I had prided myself on speaking openly, honestly and truthfully. It was about discussing the unspoken and demonstrating that so many people are in the same boat, and I had promised myself that, no matter what, I would never shy away from a direct question. I wanted my experience and the telling of my story to make a difference to people and, if I were to be true to that position and maintain credibility and the respect of the people who had contacted me, I would have to share the whole story. Dealing with the problem of the enormous debt I carry is a key part of that story.

In my view, accepting the reality that an as yet unquantified amount of both commercial and personal debt will not be repaid because of the unprecedented and dramatic change in the country's fortunes, which prohibits full repayment, is the only way that Ireland will recover in the long term. However, I realise that it's a contentious and divisive issue. When I was doing radio interviews while promoting *Shepherd's Pie*, I was a guest on a Newstalk radio show and was interviewed by Ivan Yates and Chris O'Donoghue. I was asked to share my views on the concept of debt forgiveness. Ivan Yates was having his own difficulties and facing possible bankruptcy, so he gave me quite a grilling. He seemed convinced that I was naive in thinking I could sell properties for a lesser amount than I owed on them and that the banks would write off the balance. The other interviewer, Chris O'Donoghue, then asked, 'Why should I pay for your collapse?' or words to that effect, because he had never borrowed recklessly during the Celtic Tiger years. He was furious at the prospect.

I understand that it is a difficult and emotive subject, but I believe that we must talk about it. For as long as we debate it, one side of the argument will say we need to be able to start again, to return to business, get back on our feet and be entrepreneurs creating employment again. The other side will counter this with a question: why the hell should I pay for your debt, your mistake? I didn't borrow money I couldn't repay.

I can see both sides of the argument and obviously one side is more favourable to someone in my circumstances. However, when it comes to commercial debt, I believe that the self-employed in the SME sector borrowed 'recklessly' specifically with a view to growing their business. In the process they created something, be it employment in construction or car showrooms or retail or the hospitality sector, etc. It's a fair point that not everyone borrowed so not everyone should have to repay in the form of the bailout, but in most cases the self-employed people in the SME sector who borrowed, under what it has since become clear was an unregulated and unsustainable banking and political system fuelling a false economy, did so in order to expand their business and they were, therefore, making a direct contribution to growing the economy. While I appreciate that PAYE workers and self-employed people who did not borrow such huge amounts should not be responsible for others' actions, I believe that both groups are needed to make a contribution to the economy and that you can't have one without the other. We need risk-takers and I understand that you can lose on any risk, but nobody who borrowed on the basis of the misinformation we were fed by our government and banks could possibly have hedged their bets to the extent that would have been required for them to keep their nose clean since the mid-noughties.

We laud the multinationals in this country and long may they remain here – they make a valuable contribution to local economies and pay their (lowest in Europe) corporation tax. But that's a commercial decision and, make no mistake, they're not here out of loyalty or commitment to Ireland. Even the mighty Google, out of a turnover of €12.5 billion from their Irish base in 2011, paid taxes of just €8 million.[35] Yes, the local economy benefited from the salaries of Googlers that were spent here in Ireland, but none of the profits were reinvested to growing a business in this country. The SME sector reinvests to grow and create more employment in Ireland and I believe it has been shamefully neglected by the government in its efforts to kick-start the economy and move on from the mess we have been in for five years. That is the sector of society worst hit by crushing debt and that's why I believe we need to talk about and change our attitude towards the possibility of commercial debt forgiveness. Local entrepreneurs cannot kick-start or maintain local economies while they are burdened with this problem, with no hope of ever being able to emerge from under its shadow. We need both a local and a national economy, and we need Irish people and business to fuel it. But we also need a society, and society and economy are interdependent.

According to the economist Ronan Lyons, the ten most positive things that came from the boom years in Ireland in the noughties were better roads, more healthcare resources, an educated workforce, investment in education (with spending up eighty-four per cent since 1995), the Internet economy, the services economy, higher personal incomes, fifty per cent more women joining the workforce than in 1997, 400,000

---

35 http://www.independent.ie/business/irish/google-pays-just-8m-tax-here-by-routing-9bn-profits-abroad-3251142.html

more new jobs and, finally, the experience of being an older person in Ireland, with the OEDC claiming that Ireland is one of the best places in the world to grow old.[36] As a society we have *all* benefited from the boom and that didn't happen without risk-takers as well as non-risk takers in the economy.

The banks have taken the benefit of Joe Bloggs' contribution to the bailout, but they haven't passed any of that back to Joe Bloggs so as to take some financial pressure off him, which would get him spending again and fuel the economy. That argument can also be applied to the commercially debt-ridden in the SME sector. The simple and basic, but logical, steps to the recovery of the economy in my view are:

1   Removing bank debt from the national balance sheet.
2   Triggering a systematic but managed relief of commercial debt.
3   Ditto for mortgage debt.
4   Incentives for employers to hire.
5   Reforming the social welfare system to encourage uptake of employment.

In my opinion, some form of debt relief is the key to freeing the SME struggling to trade under the weight of its debt and the emotional burden that comes with it. Any release from that pressure will result in benefits which will make their way into the economy and eventually release this country from the grips of a great depression. The existence of the Chapter 11

---

36   http://www.ronanlyons.com/2010/05/04/what-has-the-celtic-tiger-ever-done-for-us/

legislation provides for the possibility of the next American Dream in the States. Not so in Ireland. Absolutely ruling out debt forgiveness could stifle any hope of recovery. Chapter 11 has been proven to work. In Ireland we're at sea in terms of how to proceed and we need urgent legislation to formalise a process that is simpler and more effective than the Personal Insolvency Act. We don't have the resilience to bounce back, move on, forgive, like they do in one of the world's greatest economies. Perhaps we could learn a thing or two from it, like allowing second chances and punishing white-collar criminals who are responsible for collapsing economies and committing their country to decades of austerity.

Professor Jason Kilborn of John Marshall Law School in Chicago has carried out worldwide research on insolvency and bankruptcy. He has said that 'the Irish economy is already fragile, and pretending that thousands of consumers who are unable to pay their debts will miraculously be placed in a position where they can pay their debts and [that] banks will recoup what are already realistically losses, is a fantasy'.[37] Kilborn favours debt forgiveness legislation. He claims that research shows that when a financial institution is left to decide anything on a case-by-case basis, nothing happens.

I can't accept the argument that an element of debt forgiveness is unfair in Ireland considering the events of the last ten or so years. Moreover, whatever solution is agreed on for commercial debt, a formula to deal with private debt will also have to be found in the future. However, I believe that

---

37 http://www.irishtimes.com/newspaper/finance/2012/0423/1224315046485.html

attention should be turned to the pressure that is faced by mortgage holders only after we have found a mechanism for dealing with the commercial loans that are a noose around the necks of a large number of SMEs. The media seems to be particularly focused on mortgage debt, with little or no discussion about the relief of commercial debt for SMEs (other than members of the NAMA club) or how we might re-float the sinking self-employed. Ireland has re-capitalised its banks – we have written the cheque but who has received the money? The Irish taxpayer has taken the pain (self-employed or not) so why is he/she not receiving any gain in the form of an improvement in circumstances? For as long as the debt forgiveness argument keeps preventing action, we do nothing but continue to drag out this recession/depression for everyone. It is avoidance on a national scale. Hence I found myself paddling upstream in terms of trying to deal with my own debt problem, because it was clear that no legislation was imminent and that the politicians weren't even planning to properly debate the concept. I was left with no choice but to vigorously pursue a solution for myself – once again, I decided to take the issue into my own hands.

Three things had led me to the point of actively seeking debt forgiveness:

1   Making the decision to dispose of all commercial and residential investment properties.
2   Making the decision to be proactive and to engage and work with banks to become an active participant in my own recovery.
3   Meeting Tommy Murphy and Seán Dunne.

I believe that many distressed property owners are reluctant to make the decision to dump property. Maybe that's because of pride, or fear of how the bank will deal with the residual debt. Isn't that the crux of the problem? The property, the loan, the repayment, the residual debt and the bank's reaction. I have taken a view about the money that I borrowed for expansion, development or to purchase property pre- and post-2008, as well as the bank's reaction to their losses incurred because of me and the moral implication of receiving debt forgiveness. My view is that I never knowingly borrowed without intending to repay the loan in full. Pre-2008, in both my personal and commercial life, I repaid every cent I borrowed, often ahead of the term expiring. When I started to borrow in 2002 I did so in an effort to make some decent money over my lifetime in business, so that I would leave my children and their children in a strong financial position. I knew that clearing the loans I had drawn down would be a lifelong obligation that would necessitate the expansion of the business to secure this financial future, but my loans were all asset-backed with bricks and mortar. The bank was willing to lend and I was willing to borrow, under conditions that the bank imposed and that I honoured. It was a simple transaction in six easy steps:

1. Make repayments as per an agreed schedule.
2. Pay the interest.
3. Pay the margin applied by the bank.
4. Sign over the asset as security for the loan.
5. Pay all legal fees (including the bank's 'arrangement fees') to complete the purchase.
6. Sign personal guarantees if necessary.

Deal done and agreed by both parties. The deal was very specific. Fail to make the repayments and I would lose the asset regardless of any improvement I might have made to it that would increase its value. Any residual debt would be subject to the enforcement of personal guarantees, meaning they could come after my personal income and assets as well as those of the business. I understood this to be the case and so when I arrived at the point of not being able to make the repayments, I engaged with the bank to find a solution out of the three available options: (a) sell the asset; (b) lease the asset; (c) foreclosure. I was not standing in anybody's way, not obstructing the process. I was willing to honour the deal we had made.

But then the banks moved the goalposts by seeking additional security as well as more interest and, ultimately, more margin for themselves. That wasn't the deal I had signed up to. I never agreed to effectively underwrite the value of the property. Our deal never stated that if property values collapsed on a national scale I would be obliged to offer more security, or to fund the difference in the devaluation in cash. I put my deposit up front to create the initial equity and the bank agreed. They sought twenty per cent and I paid. They didn't ask for a twenty per cent deposit and increased security if the property value dropped – the deal was made in good faith.

Post-2008, with declining rental income and a substantially reduced salary, I faced huge arrears on my loan repayments, so I decided to address the issue with the bank by declaring that I couldn't service the loan repayments at their current levels. To continue to attempt to do so would threaten my mental and physical health, and I was unwilling to force my children to face the possibility of a future without their father as a result of the stress and depression that my attempts to service these loans were causing. I saw the pitfalls ahead. I knew that it would be a long and difficult road but that there would be light at the end of the tunnel so long as neither my health nor my family unity was compromised. My responsibility was to prioritise how I spent my limited income. That started with keeping a roof over my kids' heads, followed by keeping food on the table. That was my major focus in 2009 and 2010 – pure survival.

Once I had done what was necessary to ensure those basics, I turned my attention to dealing with my negative equity. House prices were down fifty per cent from the peak they had reached in 2007. The value of commercial buildings set by NAMA at approximately fifty-six per cent of their original value was now leaning towards thirty-five per cent of their original value.[38] I could see no way back from this decline. No recovery was in sight and all I could see in the future was a lifetime of struggling to pay arrears and interest on arrears. I battled to sell residential property in a market where ghost estates were being sold off for prices that meant in one case the individual houses were worth just over €10,000 each.[39] Empty and derelict car showrooms were scattered all over the country. Receiverships were so common by the middle of 2012

38   http://www.bloomberg.com/news/2012-06-12/irish-bad-bank-architect-says-agency-may-be-doomed-to-losses.html

39   http://www.independent.ie/business/personal-finance/property-mortgages/63-houses-sold-for-just-649000-but-10000-per-unit-was-four-times-the-asking-price-3166674.html

that it was hard to keep up with who owned what. Hotels, golf courses, office blocks, showrooms and a lot more were dumped in fire sales led by IBRC,[40] Royal Bank of Scotland and NAMA, each serving their own agenda and leaving a legacy of depreciating property values across the country. I had no hope, but decided that my choice would be not to waste my life fighting a war that I couldn't win.

For all my mistakes, I believe that the banks matched me step for step by failing to act, failing to deliver an urgent strategy in 2009 after the collapse of the economy and the banking system. By the time they took any action, such as setting targets for lending to SMEs or creating Consumer Protection Codes of Conduct,[41] irreparable damage had been caused. So by the time I considered the reaction of the banks to my dumping property and leaving a residual debt, I couldn't have cared less what the bank might do to me. I was ruined anyway. Every property investment I had made was in the gutter. Every share I had purchased was worthless. The banks were to get the assets, as per our deal. I would get nothing but the possibility of further exposure because of my personal guarantees, which were fairly useless because the banks had charged and cross-charged all of the properties, and the collapse of property values ruled out the use of the guarantees anyway.

---

40   After the transfer of the business of Irish Nationwide Building Society (INBS) to Anglo Irish Bank Corporation Limited on 1 July 2011, the bank's name was changed to Irish Bank Resolution Corporation Limited. IBRC was officially liquidated in February 2013.

41   http://www.centralbank.ie/regulation/processes/consumer-protection-code/pages/codes-of-conduct.aspx

I have considered the morality of not repaying in full any loans I had, as, ultimately, the Irish taxpayer is now paying. I don't believe that, morally, I've failed to fulfil my side of the deal I had with the banks – in fact, the opposite is true. I honoured my obligation by returning the assets to the bank. The reality is that banks were in deep shit because supporting documentation, security and the formulae used to establish a borrower's ability to service loans initially were flawed – none of my property deals were ever stress-tested as presumably even the banks thought that property values would only go one way, or, if they went down, the decrease would be the infamous 'soft landing' or 'correction', from which eventually equity could be gained again over time. In my opinion, banks drove the property bubble, fuelling it with easy credit to gain market share, so their risk departments developed creative methods to help borrowers overcome any barriers to a successful loan application, especially with raising funds to provide a deposit. I doubt the banks have considered the morality of that and the subsequent repercussions of it on me, either personally or as a taxpayer. However, two wrongs don't make a right, so I decided that all I could do was try my best to get as much of the loans repaid as I could and ask the banks to take their share of responsibility for the debt too.

So, having considered the magnitude of the loans, the value of their security, the banks' reactions and the moral issues, I decided to do the following:

1.   Seek the lender's permission to dispose of all properties at current market values or, failing that, have them proceed with foreclosure and take the consequences.

2. Assuming I received the banks' approval, notify them of any firm offers received, and again get their further approval to make the sale to discharge the property.
3. Only move to discharge the properties with the banks' approval, if we could agree how to handle the residual debt to both parties' satisfaction.

I arranged a meeting with Bank A, with the goal of establishing the property values and hence the potential return to the bank from selling them. The bank agreed in principle, so in 2011 I set out to get firm offers for each property. It was just one bank, but it was a start. It was a plan. I knew I couldn't face selling the properties and still have to cope with servicing residual debt into the millions, now without any assets. The bank agreed with me and, in fairness, they were very honest in explaining to me that a formula for dealing with residual debt hadn't yet been established. There were five people present at the meeting: two senior bank officials, myself, Seán and Tommy. It was a long meeting, with lots of difficult issues to address, but we got there. We managed to keep it civil and towards the end of the meeting the atmosphere was casual and friendly, as though a ceasefire had been declared and we were all now on the same side.

This relaxed mood led to a conversation that brought me to full attention. One of the bank officials said that, at some point in the future, the debt-forgiveness train would pull into the station and it would be critical for me to have a ticket to board. The official suggested that there would be crowds in the station but that many of them wouldn't have a ticket and by the time they got one, the train would have departed.

I had received an insight into the bank's view of what was required to sort out the horrible mess of debt once and for all. Mortgage debt, commercial debt, negative equity and the collapse of property values were the challenges to be addressed. The sense I got at that meeting was that two types of customer would enter the station looking to board that train and one type would end up with debt forgiveness while the other would end up with debt write-off. I asked what the difference was and that's when they explained to me that debt forgiveness could happen when a customer works with the bank to the bank's satisfaction – meaning not only a totally transparent disclosure of all assets, but also the borrower's active participation in selling or leasing the properties to gain a return from them and keep the bank's costs down. The customer would be invited to provide a detailed statement of assets which would be independently valued. Then current earnings would be assessed along with potential future earnings. When both assessments were complete, the customer would be instructed to dispose of the assets one by one.

In my case, for example, I owed just under €17 million and, if selling the assets brought in (say) €6 million, I would be faced with a residual debt of €11 million. In terms of assessing future earning capacity, as I was self-employed the bank would look not only at my salary (or specifically the bit of my salary that was left after allowing for the household budget), but also at the potential future earnings of my company, and see what I could actually manage to pay over the following thirty years. The calculation of any repayments would be such that servicing the residual debt wouldn't further threaten the day-to-day running of the business. When the calculation was complete

I could be asked to sign an affidavit confirming that I have no hidden assets or cash. Then the jigsaw would be complete. Over thirty years, based on the bank's calculations, the bank would expect to have (say) €1 million repaid of the €11 million I owed, so the balance of €10 million would be forgiven. However, this would never be put in writing. The bank suggested that, if such an agreement was made, then I would never be asked to service that balance of €10 million or interest on it, but that I would never receive written confirmation that I no longer owed it to them. So on the one hand I would have a verbal guarantee that it had been forgiven, while on the other hand there would be no written proof of such a deal. Thus, no precedent would be set and if my financial circumstances changed because I won the lottery or my new business suddenly became so successful that I was earning millions, they could still reclaim the balance of the money owed.

As a result of having nothing in writing, the customer would still bear plenty of risk. Who knows what's around the corner in this unstable economy and if circumstances changed the 'verbal agreement' could be revoked. I wondered if I made such an agreement could it somehow come back to haunt me? If the people I made such a deal with at the bank left or retired, could their replacement decide to change tack and resume the pursuit of the residual debt? It was impossible to know one way or the other what would happen in the future. However, I believed that if the chance arose it was worth taking in the interest of receiving debt forgiveness and the possibility of starting over with some peace of mind and quality of life.

Debt write-off is a different story. In that situation, a customer decides not to work with the bank, and doesn't supply accurate information or resists declaring all of their cash and assets. These are people that have, for example, properties that they have transferred to other family members, hidden cash in offshore bank accounts, or properties abroad of which there is no record with their bank in Ireland. These customers leave the bank with no option but to enforce receivership, which will ultimately leave them with no business and therefore no income from it, as well as leaving every asset that the bank is aware of up for grabs in order to call in the debt, including the family home and your dead granny's wedding ring if it has a value. The bank will leave no stone unturned to root out hidden cash or assets and will insist on a sworn affidavit that you have declared everything – if you have not, to swear an affidavit to the contrary is a criminal offence. Anyone who is in debt and not servicing their loans, and who has moved an unencumbered asset into another person's name since 2008, is likely to find themselves in court being sued by their lender and having that property moved back into their own name.

Once the bank has control of all the customer's assets, or at least the ones they know about, they will have a fire sale. This will dramatically reduce the return from the asset, so it will not provide a fraction of the return that a customer who is working with the bank to sell their own assets will get; therefore the residual debt will be much higher. When the customer has control over the sale, it is in their interest to get the best possible price and they will ensure that they do – not so if the bank is selling it off quickly. When the assets are sold, the bank will go through the same adjudication on current and potential earnings, except this time they might go to court to ensure that a proportion of earnings are paid directly to the bank for decades, regardless of the impact on the household budget, and as the business has gone into receivership there is no regard for the impact on day-to-day operations of any new business that is set up – which would be nigh on impossible to do anyway, with no access to funds. The family home would not be protected and that would form part of a fire sale of assets, although the bank would allocate some funds for the customer to buy a replacement home, one deemed to be 'appropriate' in size and location by a possibly annoyed bank official. Once everything is sold, the bank will write off the balance, but the customer will probably be left with nothing and with no prospect of starting another business or ever having access to credit again. Clearly this process is much more aggressive. Of course, the final option is for the bank to declare the borrower bankrupt.[42]

After we left the meeting that day, the three of us gathered outside the bank speechless at the lesson we had just learned. This happened in early 2010, at a time when nobody knew the banks' intentions. Needless to say, I left that meeting determined to step up my activity in trying to find buyers for my properties, work with the bank and earn debt forgiveness. I was now clear on a number of things:

1.   The bank was obviously writing the road map for dealing with their loan book. A change was imminent and they had made a distinction between three options: debt forgiveness, debt write-off and bankruptcy.

---

42   http://www.citizensinformation.ie/en/money_and_tax/personal_finance/debt/what_is_bankruptcy.html

2. I knew which option I wanted.
3. I needed a ticket for that train.
4. I had just been made privy to how an Irish bank was actively looking to move forward.

As I drove home after that meeting I couldn't fathom why the bank wouldn't go public with what they had just told me. It was a very clear strategy. It demonstrated vision and leadership. I understood it and it helped me to clear my head about what I needed to do to move forward. If they communicated this to the public, wouldn't it educate people, speed up the whole process, get the property market moving, restore confidence and prove that the bank was in fact doing something proactive to help solve the problem that they had helped create and give themselves some good press? But they weren't going public and continued with the line that each individual situation would be reviewed on 'a case-by-case basis'.

By the time I returned to the bank with a formal proposal for disposal of properties I felt my relationship with them had definitely improved. They approved my plans to dispose of each property, one by one. The next step, therefore, was to come back to them with firm offers. Months passed before the first real offer came in. In the interim I was making repayments on properties where I had a tenant. I brought the offer to the bank and they agreed to the sale at that price. I asked about the residual debt. The bank was very definite in their answer, which was that the decision to sell the property must be my own decision. The bank would not offer an opinion nor would they offer anything in writing that would confirm that any debt had been forgiven. At point the bank would say without any doubt that the outstanding balance would remain live; however, they would acknowledge that I was unable to service the debt and that into the future I would be unlikely to be able to service it. I was quite clear on the meaning. As David Trimble once said to the IRA while the peace process in Northern Ireland was ongoing, 'You jump first and we will follow.' If I was to trigger the receipt of debt forgiveness on this particular property loan, I was going to have to sign the contract for sale and hope that the bank would honour the verbal agreement not to pursue me for the balance. I believed that they would, although others thought that I needed to get something in writing at some stage to confirm that any residual debt had been forgiven. But I was under no illusion – that confirmation would never come. I had to do something. Holding on to the property would mean holding on to the debt that I couldn't service, so control over my own financial future and more importantly, my family home, could be taken from me. Knowing that made the decision a little easier when I considered my options:

Option One

Assume the bank had taken a provision on the loan and that it was greater than the residual debt on the property. Trust that they would honour the verbal agreement to reduce my debt balance. This would reduce the threat of entering a receiver-ship and it would keep me in control of the sale. Assume that the message they gave me about the residual debt was a cloaked message that said do it and we'll park the balance indefinitely.

Option Two

Not sell and see what would happen over the twelve months
that followed, in the hope that a more defined and publicly
declared process for debt forgiveness would be developed.

I decided to go for option one. I would go for it and in so
doing I would have to trust the bank. Either way it would
bring the whole issue of my burden of debt to a head, some
sort of conclusion that would allow me to get on with my life.
So, with the bank's approval I sold the first property and then
the second and then the third and so on. The bank took all of
the proceeds and no mention or reference was made to me
about the residual debt up to the end of 2012.

Then, just after Christmas 2012 I received a call from the
bank, suggesting that we meet to discuss entering into a formal
agreement to deal with the residual debt. This was the meeting
that I had been working towards for the preceding three years.
It was decision time for me and the bank. I drove to Cork
in February 2013 to hear what the bank had to say. At the
meeting it was explained to me that they were to be the first
bank in Ireland to create a programme for customers in debt,
with a formal, written policy and procedure to address debt
resolution. The bank official explained that the programme
they had designed had been approved by the Department of
Finance, the Troika and the Board of Directors of the bank.
They reckoned they were months ahead of any other financial
institution in the country in progressing a programme for
debt resolution.

The official went on to explain the process for participating
in the programme in great detail, and the more I heard, the

more I began to feel very uneasy. I quickly realised that my earlier concept of debt forgiveness for anyone who cooperated with the bank as opposed to debt write-off for those who did not, was naïve, despite the meeting I had had with the same bank some three years earlier which had suggested that there would be a seismic difference between the two. I had gone about disposing of my debt-laden assets with the understanding that my co-operation and openness with the bank would lead to an element of debt forgiveness. It was now becoming clear that that would not be the case. Either I had misunderstood or the goalposts had shifted beyond anything that I had previously discussed with the bank. I was stunned to hear the terms of the programme for debt resolution. It is a draconian programme at best, that I believe impinges on my civic rights. Everything was back on the table, including my home. The family home was no longer sacrosanct. I couldn't believe what I was hearing. I was stunned. Is it any wonder they had me sign a Non-Disclosure Agreement before the discussion?

I left the meeting feeling winded, and began mentally listing the pros and cons of the bank's proposal for me to participate in this programme. However, by now I was so committed to the process of resolving my debt that there was no turning back. The only other choice I had was to declare both myself and my wife bankrupt. That had been made very clear to me at the meeting.

Over the next few days I debated what my next move should be and thought about little else. I reflected long and hard on the debt resolution programme. I was disgusted, frustrated and angry at how I believed Bank A had misled me in 2010, when I effectively signed up to the process before it was formalised, albeit with nothing in writing, which was not my choice. The goodwill I once felt towards Bank A dissipated with this u-turn. I would like to share the details of the programme for debt resolution, to warn people and highlight the pitfalls and potential consequences, but as I have signed an NDA, I can't say anything. I can say that I welcome any debt resolution programme that offers hope for the borrower and I do accept that borrowers, and I include myself in that group, should feel some pain if they are to get a deal on debt resolution, but I fear that the programme presented to me that day contains elements that are simply over the top. The bank has made it very clear that my agreement is bespoke to my circumstances and is not a 'one size fits all' approach, but I still fear for some individuals I know who will have to face this programme. A bank that had to be bailed out by the Irish people because of their bullishness and avarice has created a solution to a problem they created which will come at a heavy cost to those people. Problem and solution, each created by a bank. Not a good combination. I fear for the mental health of those left with no choice but to participate. In my opinion, Bank A's programme for debt resolution should come with a serious health warning.

Draw your own conclusion as to whether or not I have received debt forgiveness based on these facts. My own belief is that I now know that forgiveness doesn't form part of the process. I believe that I have entered into a programme with the bank to bring about a resolution to my debt. That programme is the best possible option for both me and the bank, given the state of property values in Ireland. I have had a proportion of my debt resolved, but I will also be repaying a portion of it for many years, which I fully accept. I am a participant in a programme of debt resolution and as a result I feel relieved to have reached a conclusion about my future. Difficult as the programme is, it represents some element of action from the banks that at the very least will start the process of allowing people to consider moving forward.

I don't believe that the banks are working towards debt resolution on a case-by-case basis. That would suggest that they are assessing all distressed loans and proactively communicating with their customers about them. They are not. This I know because clients I am working with at Insight have told me that they have debt but they have not been approached. A programme of debt resolution will only be triggered when the borrower proposes a plan with which the subject can be broached. I was lucky to have had help from ACT to get my head around a possible solution to my problem, which I could take to the bank as a plan and then raise the issue of debt resolution with them.

Stopping the banks from controlling me was a turning point for me. I'm very unclear as to why the banking sector has not taken steps to announce that a debt-resolution programme is in place and, if a distressed customer were to apply to the programme, then a similar formula tailored to their particular situation but based on the same model could be applied. If used correctly, this formula would reveal any 'chancers' trying to take advantage of the programme to rid themselves of debt that they can service without selling all of their assets, but would also help expedite the recovery of so many genuine cases and thus help bring to an end what the comedian Tommy Tiernan has described as the longest funeral in history – Ireland's recession.

Even though some banks have demonstrated a willingness to move on, they seem to have failed to send that signal to their customers. I believe that customers, and I would include myself in this until recently, lack the necessary education when it comes to approaching banks to try to deal with their debt problem. Bank officials have told me that people made appointments to meet the manager in their local branch to apply for debt forgiveness as if they were applying for a loan – like they had seen an advert in a newspaper announcing that it was debt forgiveness week. That's not to say that in some cases the customer isn't very well versed in dealing with the bank, but they still would need a qualification in Morse Code to figure out whether the issue was on or off the table when discussing debt forgiveness with them. Communication from the banks on the subject is dire and the dearth of communication on it is disastrous for their credibility, in my opinion.

The public ends up reading about specific cases in the news-papers, like the case of Laura White, who secured a €152,000 write-down of her mortgage debt from Bank of Ireland in April 2012. This was one of the first recorded examples of debt forgiveness.[43] There are a number of things about that particular case that make it stand out. First of all, it wasn't a huge sum considering the debt levels that are carried by some, myself included. But also the borrower, having gone through foreclosure and having moved out of her home, was left with

---

43 http://www.independent.ie/opinion/editorial/striking-a-balance-on-debt-forgiveness-3094821.html

a residual debt of €18,000 and was repaying that at a rate of €250 per month, which continued to pin debt to the individual, restricting her disposable income. This is something that limits spending and we need people to start spending again to get the economy going. The personal insolvency bill published in the summer of 2012 would have offered Laura White the same deal without the residual balance of €18,000. It seems to me that there must have been no confidentiality agreement with her lender and so the publishing of the details of the deal may have been tactical, which demonstrates the sort of mixed messages that customers are getting about debt forgiveness – as though the bank was showing people that it was possible to secure such a deal and here's how to do it. Yet at the same time the bank in the White case could honestly say that it never offered debt forgiveness but was forced into the situation, given that it was her decision to foreclose rather than the bank's. This allows the bank to crystallise its loss but also to protect itself by saying that there is no programme in place that offers any customer debt forgiveness.

I believe that such mixed messages are prolonging people's misery from year to year. It's a tough subject but it's on the tough subjects that we need real leadership and strategy focused not only on mortgage debt but also on commercial debt – Ireland needs its business brains working. It needs all of its entrepreneurs, small and large. It doesn't need a banking sector controlling the economy. It doesn't need its boardrooms filled with receivers, civil servants and bank officials.

Laura White's legal team argued that the bank should have given her permission to dispose of the property earlier and that, because of their refusal to act sooner, the property had declined in value as the economy worsened, increasing her exposure and ultimately costing the taxpayer. This was exactly the same for me on five investment residential properties that I owned. I sought permission to sell the five of them in 2009 expecting to get €1 million for all five combined, having paid €1.275 million for them, but was refused. In 2012 I approached the bank again for permission to sell the houses and got it, but this time I projected sales revenue from all five combined of just €700,000. This has been the case all over the country. Property will not recover its value so long as NAMA are organising auctions of distressed properties.

Customers should understand that the banks don't necessarily have all the rights on their side any more. There is a strong case emerging for a rebalancing of the relationship between the borrower and the lender because everything has changed so dramatically. We live in unprecedented times in banking. Whatever deals you did as a borrower, whatever interest you agreed to pay and whatever security you gave, you would be wise to review it all, because when you signed up, it was a different era. Things are moving and changing weekly. I know of quite a few cases that are currently with the Ombudsman because wording on documents changed slightly when loans were reviewed and new sanction letters were issued under the heading of 'Interest', given what the bank deemed to be the increased risk profile of the borrower. The Ombudsman wouldn't take on those cases without due cause.

In July 2012 the *Irish Examiner* reported that businessman David Walsh was refunded €33,000 in interest and had the repayments on his commercial loan reduced by €30,000 annually. The report from the Ombudsman confirmed that Bank of Ireland had breached Mr Walsh's rights in a number of ways. This is just one example of someone successfully turning the gun back on the bank and there are plenty of these cases out there. But we need to be proactive and not reactive about it and do it in greater numbers.

On 29 July 2012 (the day before Mr Walsh's verdict hit the headlines) I was a guest speaker at an event that had been organised to show support for Seán Quinn. My role was not directly to support Quinn, but to talk about banking in Ireland and to demonstrate that there were good banks as well as bad banks. At the rally I was told how many local business owners were terrified about going up against not just their own bank but the establishment and especially IBRC (Anglo). It was quite shocking to me to learn that people were so frightened, but I presume that's why I had been invited to speak. However, now we're seeing cases like Laura White and David Walsh, which I see as the green shoots of the people fighting back. As a people we need to do more to take banks on and reveal their errors, which are costing us and prolonging this miserable time in the story of Ireland. We know from those two cases at least that banks are not standing on perfect ground. Start picking away. Start investigating. Apply your own pressure, but engage. Ask questions on everything that you don't understand and don't lose sight of the fact that when you borrowed the money, day one, you had a deal. You got the money and they got the property if it all went pear-shaped. Don't give any more security. Just say no and refer back to the original agreement. Don't give in and don't be swayed by slick marketing and advertising campaigns showing the caring side of a bank that wants to help you, communicate with you and work with you to rebuild. Absolute horse shit. If the banking sector was sincere in that message, they should start by communicating in a far clearer manner what they want customers to do, and let them know that they are willing to discuss a programme of debt resolution if that is what is required for a business or personal recovery.

As for me, I am in a programme of debt resolution which likely means that millions of euro will never be repaid. But I won't walk away scot-free. I have lost the property portfolio that I paid big deposits on from my own cash reserve built up over years of hard work. Those properties were my pension. I will have paid a small fortune to the banks in interest, fees, charges and margin along the way. I will be servicing a long-term residual debt for many years into the future and my ability (and desire) to ever borrow again has been destroyed, which may impede growth in my business. On the other hand, I believe that I honoured my end of the agreements I had to the best of my ability and that I did not walk away until an acceptable resolution was found. I worked with the bank up to the very end. It has cost me the failure of three businesses and the process has hurt many, including my wife and parents. So yes, my debt has been reduced but I'm not walking away smiling. I thank God that I have arrived at this point because the burden of debt and the conflict I was experiencing with banks could have tipped me over the edge. I have managed to eliminate both, but not without personal pain. I still ponder what might have been – especially when I'm stuck in traffic and see stickers in rear windows of cars that were purchased in one of my closed dealerships. I'm sad to say though that since then many more dealerships have gone the same way as mine did.

I was very nervous writing this chapter. My intention when writing it was to convey my view that Ireland must deal with the issue of debt and take the pain of writing off an element of both commercial and personal debt for the economy to recover – our collective end game must be economic recovery for all our sakes and that of future generations. Whatever your view on debt forgiveness, this is our new reality. I know that because I've experienced it. People should be allowed a second chance and the banking and political sectors could provide a format or structure to facilitate this in a more fluid manner. Banks have a responsibility to participate in recovery as they had such a huge role in the demise of the economy, and so they have a moral obligation to engage with their customers and communicate their strategies openly.

Finally, in my experience there is no real debt forgiveness in the literal meaning of the expression. I have not been absolved of my debt or the consequence of not being able to repay it. I have accepted my fate and continue to work towards a resolution of my debt, despite the fact that that wasn't the agreement I signed up to. I can't pretend it never happened because I'm living with the consequences and everywhere I look I see constant reminders of the past ten years. Writing this chapter was a challenge. It was difficult. But if sharing how I arrived at the solution that worked for me helps someone else achieve a result that works for them, I'm happy with that.

Key Lesson: Review all the paperwork you have relating to your loan agreements. Understand that when you entered into the agreement with your lender(s) you had a contract that cannot be altered – you got the money, they got the property if you couldn't repay. The value of the security on it is irrelevant. Work with banks with the goal of avoiding having a receiver appointed. If you propose a plan that includes a programme of debt resolution which is acceptable to the bank, it is highly unlikely that you will receive any confirmation in writing. Research the Personal Insolvency Bill.[44] Make long-term decisions – think pension and age profile. Don't just settle for the here and now. Deals are being done daily to give people a second chance, and you could get a second chance too.

---

44   http://www.justice.ie/en/JELR/Pages/PR12000198

8

Men in dark suits

If you want one year of prosperity, grow grain, if you want ten years of prosperity, grow trees. If you want one hundred years of prosperity, grow people.

Chinese Proverb

When I was invited to speak at the now infamous rally to support Seán Quinn in Ballyconnell in July 2012, I was told that, regardless of whether I agreed or disagreed with his actions, I could speak freely. I knew it would attract huge media attention so I saw it as an opportunity to talk about tackling the banks and how to kick-start recovery. The organisers were anxious that I attend and so they sent a helicopter to collect me – I'm not sure who paid for that. I lined out with Fr Brian Darcy, Mickey Harte, Seán Boylan and others. I told the 5,000 people assembled that there are good, bad and ugly banks and called on banks to open up and start communicating with their customers about exactly what is required for both parties to move on. The media who were there chose to report on the celebrities who attended, slating them for supporting Quinn, rather than take up the message I had tried to communicate, which was disappointing. I met members of the Quinn family, which was awkward because I had been critical of their actions in the past, but, to their credit, they accepted that I was trying to communicate a message that was not about them personally. I made the point that, notwithstanding the allegations about Quinn's dealings with Anglo, the IBRC had removed one of the most natural entrepreneurial talents ever seen in the history of Irish corporate life.

I strongly believe that the banking crisis in Ireland has quietly shifted from being a serious liquidity problem to something far more damaging for the economy. It may sound dramatic, but it's fair to say that banks are controlling the economy with frequent appointments of receivers and liquidators in order to cut their losses, and this has a knock-on effect throughout the economy. Such appointments give the bank day-to-day control over a business and whatever assets are held by it, which usually results in a fire sale of the assets and the removal of the entrepreneur from their business, often overnight. An economy controlled by indecisive banks is not good for the future of the country, not good for business and not good for property values. To say that someone like me has made a pig's ear of things because of the debt I took on is an understatement, no question. But over the next decade, who is best placed to resolve that mess? Is it dark-suited accountants appointed by banks who have little or no relevant experience and don't have a clue about my business, or me, with the drive and determination I have to recover and succeed? Who polices the receiver's activity? How does anyone know whether they are working to save the business, to wind it down, or working only towards finding a buyer? How much are they paid for the service and how is that decided? If entrepreneurs were left in control, they would work to repay their agreed debts while protecting the laying hen – the trading entity. At that rally for the Quinns in Cavan, I was asked by the organisers to announce that over €400 million in fees had been stripped from the Quinn business for the men in dark suits. The consequences of receiverships affect us all and further delay Ireland's economic recovery.

It seems to me that since 2008 Ireland's banks have been slowly removing the entrepreneurial talent from business in this way, throwing some very experienced business people on the scrap heap because of the unprecedented events of the last five years. It is devastating for all concerned and reckless in the long term, especially when some decisions to appoint receivers seem to be more aligned to the bank's long-term strategy than to that of the person who owns the business. Given the enormous debt that banks in this country owe the Irish people, it is unfathomable that the government has not moved to protect indigenous Irish taxpayers, businesses and entrepreneurs. Reckless lending and borrowing got us into this mess. The people have paid for the mess so the government should ensure that the banks pay it forward. Instead the banks are increasing interest rates, personal banking fees and not communicating their plan for dealing with mortgage arrears and commercial debt to those people who bailed them out – and that is creating a whole new banking crisis in Ireland.

If you fear that the appointment of a receiver to your business is on the horizon, I think you should consider the following as a matter of urgency:

1. Who owns the building you are trading from, you or your company?

2. If it is your own rather than the company's, does the company have a lease with you as the landlord, which protects the company as a tenant and, if so, is the lease due for renewal any time soon? The longer the lease, the better. If the company is a tenant, it cannot be removed from the property even if a receiver is appointed.

3. How robust is the lease in terms of formality, legality and duration?

4. If you don't have a lease, can you create one quickly?

5. If the company owns a premises, examine the original documentation you signed that allows the bank to take the premises as a security against any other borrowings. Check that the documentation will stand up to a robust examination by an independent security expert and if it doesn't stand up to such scrutiny, challenge the bank's entitlement to hold it as security; this could protect the premises and allow you to continue trading from it.

6. Understand any additional security while also under-standing the difference between a floating charge or a debenture. This will explain if your fixtures and fittings and stock are charged. If not you might very well find that you hold a little more leverage with the receiver, in that they might hold the keys to the building but noth-ing inside, such as furniture, equipment etc.

7. Carefully read the wording around the appointment of a receiver on the terms and conditions of the paperwork for the loan. Are you entitled to notice? Can the receiver force a sale? If you own the building and no charge has been taken over the fixtures and fittings or stock, the receiver must negotiate with you on these issues as it will complicate a sale if you still own the fixtures and

fittings, which will be in your favour. In other words, the locks can't be changed overnight to keep you out and unable to trade.

8. If at all possible, don't assign any rental income to the bank because if you do you will lose your ability to negotiate future tenancies and rents.

Some or all of these considerations may be of no help at all in your situation and it's impossible to cover all scenarios, but my point is that, given the prevalence of the appointment of receivers by the banks, business owners must act to understand where they are vulnerable if a bank decides on that course of action with their business. Understanding the ownership of assets and the security held on the loans for them is key.

There are plenty of people trading from premises they own but on which they have no formal lease, and they are in arrears on the mortgage for the premises. However, they are still trading, so have the ability to earn an income. Thus if the bank moves to foreclose on the building, the livelihood is also gone. If you're in this situation, get a lease urgently. Another big issue for business tenants all over the country is that they might have a healthy business which is trading away and doing OK, but might not be aware that their landlord is in trouble with arrears on their property. In this instance, if the tenant doesn't have a lease, they are in danger of being removed from the premises by any receiver appointed to the landlord, which could ruin a healthy business – make sure you have a lease, whatever your circumstances. You can't be removed from a premises by a receiver if you hold a proper lease and, in fact, if it is your own building the lease could put you in a strong position to negotiate with a receiver. They might have to buy you out. They might ask you to take over the security and maintenance of the full building at a reduced rent, saving themselves a load of work and cost. Don't get caught without a lease and ensure that you are paying some kind of rent consistently, even if it's in arrears.

In my own struggle for survival in business, I called the use of such tactics street fighting, and had to use some of them just to hang on for as long as I could. During the height of my distress in 2009/2010, I thought of going to work on a daily basis as going to war. I saw it as climbing into the trench to continue my fight, and this was before I had the clarity of mind to ask the 'what are you prepared to do' question. I was street fighting on instinct at that stage and regularly met with my solicitor to discuss different tactics that might help protect my family and business from hostile banks, while staying on the right side of the law. That became incredibly frustrating because, if I had an idea and wanted the legal view about whether or not I could act on it, I was generally advised to 'sit on the fence'. It was maddening, but it was also another factor that led me to decide that I was on my own and would have to do my best to inform myself and act accordingly, in the full knowledge that I could very easily fail – but taking comfort from the fact that I would go down fighting if that happened.

By late 2011 it was clear that receiverships were not working and that banks and business owners would need to find alternative solutions to facilitate recovery. Receiverships had resulted in empty buildings all over the country. Receivers then had to appoint security firms to protect the empty buildings, along with maintenance firms. Fees for these services started to mount up. The properties were not selling so fire sales commenced, which compounded declining property values, further exacerbating the banks' problems, which in turn continued to impede economic recovery. There have been occurrences of former property owners standing up at fire sale auctions asking people not to bid on their former property as it had been lost to a receiver.[45] It is soul-destroying to watch the former owner of a house or premises see the result of their life's work auctioned off in a two-minute sale. I hope never to have to experience it myself.

Ireland is in the grip of a second, less obvious crisis. The removal of vast amounts of experience from the SME sector because of receivers being appointed to struggling businesses is short-sighted. There seems to be little or no consideration of the impact of this on the greater economy, property values, families and communities. Banks shutting businesses down doesn't benefit the taxpayer and seems to only serve the purpose of the banks in terms of writing down their loan book and crystallising their loss. Why not execute a strategy to crystallise losses but in such a way that a business can continue to trade? What will be left of indigenous Irish business when all of this is washed out? Will the banks be running our businesses? I fear the answer to that question.

I believe that there is only one possible sliver of hope if a receiver is appointed to your business, which is that you might (depending on your situation) get an opportunity to deal directly with them and try to negotiate. If you get that

---

45   http://www.independent.ie/business/personal-finance/property-mortgages/familys-joy-as-daughter-buys-back-house-taken-over-by-bank-3116945.html

opportunity, at the very least you will (probably) be dealing with a commercially minded person and not a bank official. There will be none of the baggage that may exist in a long relationship with your bank manager and you will have an objective view of your business. According to insolvency specialists Kavanagh Fennell, corporate receiverships rose by twenty-six per cent from 2010 to 2011 and 'the level of corporate receiverships is running at unprecedented levels'.[46] The research also notes a new trend – share receiverships, as seen in the Quinn Group, where a receiver is appointed over the shares of a company in an effort to keep the company trading but under the stewardship of the receiver. I find that very worrying. I would favour a creative alternative such as shared responsibility, where the owner is kept on and retains a smaller percentage of the company, but continues to control the day-to-day under the guidance of a board of directors which includes some of the creditors.

Our media talks about how worrying it is that we are losing some of our best young talent to emigration. I think that the danger of losing our best corporate talent is just as worrying and potentially more damaging to our economic recovery. This situation is unlikely to change any time soon and so it is more important than ever before that we support and encourage the next generation of Irish entrepreneurs – of which there were many fine examples in the 2012 Ernst & Young 'Young Entrepreneur of the Year' competition. I sincerely hope that our mistakes at the very least serve to

---

46 http://www.kavanaghfennell.ie/news/overview/12-04-23/Insolvency_trends_and_outlook_for_2012_-_An_Irish_perspective.aspx

educate the next generation and that the men in dark suits are kept at bay.

Key Lesson: Do whatever is necessary and possible to protect what's important. Don't fall asleep at the wheel. Be proactive with trying to stay in control of your business affairs – try a creative solution with your creditors. Better that you control your affairs than a receiver.

9

Cornflakes in the shape of Jesus

A CD. How quaint. We have these in museums.

Eoin Colfer, The Eternity Code

By August 2012 my relationship with ACT in a service/ client capacity had ended and we had been working together voluntarily and interdependently for eight months. By then my advice service, Insight, was up and running, and word of mouth and an online presence provided all the marketing that I needed. I had referred many of the people from all over Ireland who had contacted me via Insight, which is a one-to-one counselling service based on shared experience rather than a professional qualification, to ACT, which offers professional advice and practical solutions. After someone had contacted me, I would generally brief Seán and Tommy on the specifics of an individual's circumstances, with their permission of course, and then the person would meet ACT for a cup of coffee, which may or may not lead to a professional evaluation and action plan. ACT sometimes kept me informed of the person's progress and would occasionally ask me to attend some meetings to assist.

I find the work I do both with Insight and with ACT very rewarding. I had no idea that the path I embarked on having delivered a manuscript for *Shepherd's Pie* could possibly result in the journey I took over the following eighteen months, ultimately arriving at this destination.

The key business message that I wanted to convey in the telling of that story, aside from the trials and tribulations of family business and the emotional correction I went through after the collapse of the business, was that creativity and planning for the future are key to the survival of any business in mid- or post-recession Ireland. By the third quarter of 2012, my business was largely unrecognisable from what it had been fourteen months earlier, but it was back on track and I felt in control of my own destiny. My brother and I, along with Seán and Tommy, had worked damn hard to make it so, between dealing with the banks, restructuring the business and finding a new business model to replace the broken one. I think that the three most important considerations at a strategic level when planning a road map for recovery in an SME in Ireland are:

- Creativity
- Research & Planning
- Decisiveness

I believe these three items to be critically important and that the lack of one or all of them, as part of a strategy for survival or recovery, has destroyed some excellent businesses. Banks might park your debt, they might sanction fresh capital or you might have the best financial advice in the world, but if you fail to be creative, plan, research and make decisions to move forward, I think the business is doomed. As I mentioned in an earlier chapter, I regularly allow myself time to reflect and, on reflection, I would say that the top ten steps I took towards recovery were:

1. The emotional correction – finding the will to fight, driven by the desire to survive.
2. Understanding that my reaction to the banks and the recession was part of my problem.
3. Gaining clarity and belief in what is really and crucially important in my life.
4. Sharing my story – for me this involved writing *Shepherd's Pie.*
5. Climbing out of my ivory tower and re-engaging with my customers.
6. Creating www.wesourceNEcar.com. If I had stuck with the old business model, it would have been over for the business.
7. Meeting Seán and Tommy and engaging with the banks.
8. Making tough decisions that sometimes neither my wife, my business partner and brother Brian, nor ACT agreed with.
9. Terminating the franchise relationships.
10. Learning how to do online marketing and business development.

Each of those ten steps was fuelled by either creativity, research or decisiveness. There is no quicker way to fix your business than to create footfall by stimulating customer interest, and the only way to do that successfully is to stand out, be different, offer something more or something better, and then communicate that message to potential customers. If you're in business and you have managed to hang on in there up to this point, your business may well be wounded, but at least it still has a beating heart. In that case you are in a position where you can decide to take responsibility for your recovery, move forward and start the slow process of rebuilding your customer base, your turnover and your profit.

I was online one evening in February 2012, doing research for a presentation, when it dawned on me that the iPhone was less than five years old. I was astonished, because to me it feels like the iPhone has been around for so much longer. It has become a lifeline for me personally – email, Internet, phone, music and so much more. I have come to depend on it completely for both my business and personal life. That got me thinking about other advances in technology that people now depend on – iPad, Facebook, Twitter, Skype, YouTube, Google, Netflix, digital TV, GPS and so on. And this progress is not limited to technology. There were fantastic strides in medicine in 2011, including bionic contact lenses, a cancer vaccine that has reduced cancerous tumours by eighty per cent in tests,[47] and 'glowing tumours', albeit still in the experimental phase, where aminolevulinic acid makes tumours glow under UV light during surgery.[48] While you and I and our neighbours and families have been stuck under this rock of misery called recession, life has gone on and the world has been moving on. The advances being made could leave us behind if we don't rise above the recession and keep up.

---

47   http://www.medicalnewstoday.com/articles/239115.php
48   http://www.bbc.co.uk/news/health-15521102

We have been so focused on survival that the brutal truth for many of us is that it won't be the recession which takes us down, it will be our lack of knowledge, our lack of understanding the digital age and what's coming next that will destroy our businesses. I see three-year-old children taking Mummy's phone, sliding their tiny thumb over the release bar, clicking on their favourite game and playing it. I see my kids take photos with phones and upload them to virtual albums. I follow my daughter on Twitter. I see people reading sports news on their smartphone in Tesco while they are shopping. I buy cars from the UK by clicking on the 'chat with an advisor' tab on a website from my phone. Lifestyle change has accelerated because of technological advances and our children will grow up never knowing an alternative. Think of a child in sixth class in an Irish primary school today. The digital knowledge that they will have in five or ten years, together with new advances in technology, will blow us away. Assuming a full second and third-level education follows, those kids will be in the workplace by around 2020. I will be fifty-four and I hope I'll still be working and running my business. Will I be able to keep pace with those kids? Employer or employee, business or leisure, we'll all have to keep pace.

A five-year time frame up to 2012 saw the invention of the iPhone. Imagine what further advances humankind will make in the time frame to 2017; where will Ireland be by then? What do you need to do in your business to keep up – considering that many parts of this country still don't have high-speed Internet access? We are losing that battle in Ireland. Many businesses don't even have a website, or if they do it's merely an online presence and doesn't capture any business. I think that the importance of using the Internet to drive your business into the future cannot be stressed highly enough. It gives you access to customers who would never otherwise find you and who consume in a new way – online.

This point was never clearer to me than when I got a phone call in 2012 from a guy who had heard about www.wesourceNEcar.com and said that he fancied a six-month-old BMW 520 in white. I said, 'That will be €38,000,' and he said, 'OK let's do it, here's my Visa card number to pay the deposit.' The motor industry is unique, in that trust in the salesperson or dealership is often the biggest selling point, especially when dealing with a used car. So if you can get an Irishman who you have never met, hasn't seen the car, hasn't kicked the tyres, hasn't test-driven it and has never set foot inside your dealership before to make the second biggest purchase of his life after his home (for the average person) online, then you have an idea of the opportunities the Internet provides. And the consumer that it attracts is diverse.

Compare, for example, an Irish buyer with a British buyer in the market for a used car in the traditional way. Typically a UK dealership will base its sales pitch on detail such as the presentation of the car, the forecourt layout, the service history and the price. The price will be tested daily against the competition online. The car will be in mint condition – the roads in Britain are better maintained and so do less damage to cars. The layout of the forecourt will be organised to offer the customer a range of vehicles displayed by either price or brand, and the service history is a very important part of the decision to purchase. Failure to have a clearly displayed service history and service book will likely cost the dealer the sale. But the prices will rarely if ever be open to negotiation. The price you pay is the price displayed. In Ireland it's different. The service book is rarely maintained with any care and the quality of the cars is not as good because of our roads. The forecourt display is disorganised in most cases and the price is so negotiable that the first €1000 is often discounted within the first minute of negotiation. The customer must touch, drive and examine the car before buying, so to ever imagine that we could get people to buy a car over the phone, having sourced online without either of us ever having seen it, might seem impossible.

It isn't. We now have the first virtual car sales business in Ireland and word of mouth is spreading the message, as well as online marketing and customer satisfaction. This has resulted in customers contacting us who already understand the concept before we have to explain it. If someone is trawling the Internet looking for a particular used car, we can help. There is a short video in the website that explains the service we provide. We do all the running and racing for people who don't have time to shop around but want to, so they tell us what car they want and at what price and we will find the car or the nearest alternative to it for them. Our sales approach and the concept are unique and that in itself attracts leads – any business will fail without new leads that turn into new customers. Think about your own workplace. Is it cutting edge? Does it stand out for excellence in the marketplace that you compete in, or is it laced with complacency, old style, no drive and no fresh thinking? If it's the latter, what can you do to change that and make yourself a more valuable employee or a self-employed person whose future is secured?

The lack of understanding of this fundamental point was made very clear to me recently when I was out for a drink. My wife and I were in a long established pub that seems to have lost a lot of customers and is not as busy as it once was. It's a beautiful premises, but the staff seem disinterested and demotivated, which is a big no-no in the service industry. As it happened, we were chatting about this chapter of the book and how so many people are losing their way in business because they are either complacent or stuck in a time warp, when our drinks arrived with half melted ice, no lemon, no coaster and water-marked glasses. We looked around the pub. It was 9 p.m. on Saturday night. There was no music. No ambient lighting. No comfortable chairs. Dead. And there on the table was our drink, looking very miserable and uninviting. Here was a business that had lost its way.

Ireland's recession has turned plenty of people into prophets of doom, exhausted and washed out by it all, who feel no hope and have given up trying. I can't accept that. There are people who are making money in Ireland during this recession. Plenty are thriving or successfully starting over. In the last five years my business world has changed dramatically as a result of the crisis but also because of technology and my increased or better use of it. Lack of creativity, research, decisiveness has a part to play in the negativity about Ireland's future. There's no place for complacency in the SME sector now and there are opportunities to grow online. The range of consumer goods available to purchase online is staggering. Your own inflatable church for your wedding? No problem. A small tub of uranium to whiten your teeth? Easy. A Russian tank with full service history? A see-through canoe? Owl vomit, snake venom or scorpion poison? Or my personal favourite, cornflakes in the shape of Jesus? It's all there at the push of a button. I remember when you couldn't find pasta in Irish supermarkets. There has been a seismic shift in lifestyle because of the availability of consumer goods online as well as on the high street, which means that businesses and business models have to change to survive.

Here are a few things to consider that illustrate how real and tangible this point is:

Supermarkets' online shopping and delivery allows you to grocery shop from your own home.

Question: Would you consider opening a grocery store?

Newspapers and books can be downloaded, or news received from many websites.

Question: How will the erosion of print affect the future of the printer/newsagent/publisher/distributor and associated businesses?

Apple TV, iTunes, Netflix, Digital Playback, etc., provide immediate entertainment.

Question: Would you open a DVD rental or music shop now?

Online banking, bill payments and loan applications have seen reduced numbers employed in banks and branches closed.

Question: What's the future of the high-street bank?

Flights, package holidays, hotels, tickets, etc., are all easily booked directly online.

Question: How will high-street travel agents be affected over the next five years?

Online gambling has revolutionised the gaming industry, with people making a full-time living from it and playing in games all over the world from their own home.

Question: If you are a bookie who has not developed online, do you believe your declining sales are purely a result of the economic downturn?

All of the activities described above can be carried out using one device. Technology is a way of life and its use will increasingly affect the way we run our lives. Don't miss the boat.

Our world is changing and so are our customers. In 2010 more than 140,000 new broadband subscriptions were logged by ComReg, bringing the grand total of broadband users in Ireland to 1.59 million.[49] That's a staggering domestic market to have access to via the Internet. Online shoppers in Ireland spent a total of €4 billion in 2011, up from €2.96 billion in 2010. This trend is set to continue with growth of up to thirty-nine per cent a year. The online shopping market in Ireland is set to reach €21 billion by 2017. Clothes and sports goods remain the second most popular items bought online, after travel deals and hotel bookings. Up to seventy-five per cent of that money will be spent on items that will be shipped into

---

49   http://www.iia.ie, 'State of the Net', Issue 21, Summer 2011

Ireland, which indicates that Irish businesses are not reaping the rewards of this growth because they are not equipped to do business online.[50] I realise now that if I had not stepped back, done the research and made the tough decisions, I would have ultimately failed in business. Recovery as things were was not possible. I believe that whatever business you're in you have to research, travel to experience different markets if possible and do more than just have a presence online.

Recession can be devastating both personally and in business and the speed with which the Irish economy collapsed left many people reeling, but it camouflaged a digital explosion that is changing how we buy and sell, how we communicate, how we educate, how we research, how we entertain and how we relax. I believe that I have engaged with technology to drive my business forward as best I can for now, but I won't rest on my laurels. I will travel to Hong Kong and California purely for research and hope to bring home three or four ideas that can grow the business of The Mordaunt Group as well as ideas that might attract adolescents to Get Your Locks Off, all the while keeping one eye on consumer trends that might help Anne's boutique business.

My decision to give up on new car franchising was made after I attended the Paris motor show in 2010. While I was there I didn't look at cars. I watched what cars the visitors flocked to. I saw demand for European cars, not Japanese cars. The greener the better, that's what people wanted. Activity around the stands of European and particularly German

---

50   http://www.independent.ie/national-news/online-spend-at-4bn-a-year-but-75pc-of-it-is-going-abroad-3258911.html

brands such as Audi, VW, Skoda and BMW was staggering compared to Japanese brands such as Nissan and Toyota. The competitive advantage that Japanese cars had held in the 1990s and 2000s was being eroded and the styling of Japanese cars was falling behind. At that show in Paris I saw the future and realised that I would need to put myself in a position where I could sell all types of cars, not just Nissan or Toyota, otherwise I was limiting my customer base. No one can afford to do that. The nonsense of spending millions on a showroom and then limiting myself to a small percentage of the car-buying public, ignoring the other ninety-four per cent who chose cars other than the brands I stocked, became so obvious – and disastrous. I decided it would be a far more sustainable business if I stopped counting on the 100,000 or so people who change their new car every three years, and instead concentrated on capturing the attention of the 1.8 million used-car owners who would eventually want a change, by offering them an unlimited range of brands.[51] That in itself would increase my sales leads exponentially, and it was over to my skills as a salesman after that. But without an interested customer, I had nothing.

So, in the interest of a self-audit of where you stand with the use of technology in your business and how you might be able to use it better to secure the future of your business, consider the following:

1. What are the challenges to my business over the next five years?

---

51   http://www.simi.ie/Statistics/National+Vehicle+Statistics.html

2. How will technology impact the industry I am in over the next five years?

3. Am I doing enough to keep pace with technology changes?

4. What is a natural fit to bolt onto my business to increase sales?

5. Does my business stand out? What is its USP?

6. Do I proactively communicate with my customers?

7. Am I trying to reinvent the wheel? If so, why?

8. When last did I travel for research and ideas?

9. Am I still blaming the recession for my continuing decline in turnover?

10. Am I the dead anchor or the beating heart of my business?

11. Is my business being left behind? How can I tell?

12. Is my company website merely an online presence?

By late 2012 I found that I could probably do with hiring again, just to ensure that I could follow up and attempt to capture a sale from the level of sales leads that were coming in. I battled with the idea of employing more staff, but I had learned my lesson about locking myself up in an ivory tower and have kept the promise I made to myself to remain at the heart of my business, so I made the decision not to. Eighty per cent of our sales leads come directly to me and I allocate the leads to one of three sales people. Either Brian or myself source all of the cars. I speak to every customer who makes an online purchase to ensure they get what they want, build trust and ensure that both customer and vendor are happy with the deal before money exchanges hands. We keep things very tight and carry no baggage or bad habits from the old ways and the old business model. I won't make the same mistakes again. I am fully in control this time and don't plan on screwing it up. I feel confident in the way we are handling emerging trends and in the way that we have stripped everything back to absolute basics. I hear about dealerships still embroiled in the new-car business almost knifing each other for the next deal under horrendous pressure from distributors hounding them for numbers, and can honestly say I don't miss it, neither the grief nor the politics of it. As I listen to those horror stories I sympathise, but thank God that I changed course and think to myself, small is beautiful.

Key Lesson: Consider the questions: What do you need to do to increase sales and profitability, other than cost-cutting which you have probably already done? Do you stand out? What is your online business activity? If you don't have any, get creative and think of a way to get your business online to find more customers. Plan. Research. Be bold. Be decisive. In your world be the shepherd rather than the sheep.

10

White-water rafting

Do not wait for your ship to come in – swim out to it.

Unknown

I have gone through a huge learning curve in both my personal and business life since the beginning of the economic crisis in Ireland. I continue to learn as a result of my work with Insight. I meet so many different people, characters and personality types in the course of the work I do there. People have educated me. Their stories have touched me and moved me to tears at times. Talking to people, sharing experiences and information and that feeling of being in the trenches together can give a person an invaluable perspective and spark change in both parties. I can see immense changes in my own character, hopefully for the better. I have become far more active, mentally, physically, verbally. I am a high-energy person now, with a zest for life and an appreciation of what's really important for me to be a happy and fulfilled human being, which I remember daily. That's not to say that I have total control over my thoughts, emotions and behaviour if I feel overwhelmed or intimidated or allow the negativity of the prophets of doom to bring me down. I wish I did, but even though I can't control the first thought that occurs to me as an immediate reaction to anything, I can certainly control the second one and that gives me the choice of how I want to proceed – I won't let the bastards drag me down! So I have decided that I am an active participant in both my financial rescue and in my own life. But it took time to arrive at this conclusion, to train my mind into thinking this way and to change my behaviour to make it real.

It all started over a meal that I had with Tommy from ACT after another long day at the office, reviewing management accounts and shooting the breeze on banking issues and economic recovery generally. By that point, the ACT guys had been working with me on my business recovery for fifteen months and together we had succeeded far beyond anything that I could have imagined or hoped for. The conversation continued over dinner and eventually came around to the idea that we had frequently bandied about (before I set up Insight) – how we could continue the work we were doing but share the information and learning to help others with their recovery, or at least let them know that recovery is possible. ACT were assisting people facing financial ruin daily, which naturally became hugely stressful for them personally at times. But over many late nights after long days, I listened carefully to the descriptions of situations where clients were taking the tough decisions and moving forward, and others where success was not yet on the horizon because a client was still sitting on the fence of indecision. Thankfully, as a client of ACT I fell into the former category, but Tommy explained that some of their clients never let go of the resistance I had felt towards both him and Seán after the initial introduction, and that in itself can stall the client's ability to move forward. In contrast, I grew to view them as additional members of my management team, which is very much the aim of their business. Seeing them as external consultants in my view would have been counter-productive, so in my business they were involved at management level and took part in discussions about every problem, including previous months' performances, and were part of the consensus required to make any business decisions.

I realise that this is more difficult to swallow for some personality types than for others, especially amongst the self-employed who are protective and territorial about their own business and are slow to allow others to influence any part of it. I was so jaded and without hope that I didn't have that issue. Any help at all was welcome and I trusted them instinctively because they had the credentials and experience and I respected their no-bullshit attitude. I also knew that I was strong enough to disagree and call a halt to anything that I wasn't comfortable with if needed – and I frequently did.

That evening, over dinner, Tommy told me a story that demonstrated exactly what it is they do and how they help business people in financial trouble, in the context of our chat about how we could extend the work we were doing together. He described his experience of a white-water rafting trip he had once taken in Canada. The guide on the trip had told the group as they were about to get into the raft, having put on their helmets, that if any of them fell out of the raft while going through the swirling rapids they must be an active participant in their own rescue. Their guide and their fellow rafters would try to help get them back on board, but if they were passive they could not be rescued, no matter what anyone else tried to do to help.

When I heard that story it was like somebody turned on a light in my head. Maybe it was a very basic concept, but for me it was the final piece of the jigsaw. I needed to become an active participant in my own rescue. I had been doing this all along, but unwittingly, really just taking on board what ACT were advising me to do. I had been fighting to survive as a reaction to the fear of not knowing an alternative. Now I am fighting to survive with the knowledge that unless I am active in my own rescue, I cannot be rescued. That has made all the difference to my ability to control any negativity or be dragged down and feel hopeless again.

When I meet people now, either informally or through Insight, I find myself sizing up their character and circumstances to take a view on whether they are or can become active participants in their own rescue. The truth is that very few are and some never will be unless they too experience that light bulb moment. The conversation on that night changed everything for me. That was the piece that had been missing. That was the key. That was the message I thought needed to be communicated to any self-employed person who was struggling. Whenever I travelled around Ireland to speak at an event or a conference, I told this story and it always got a tangible reaction – I could almost see the room flood with light from all those light bulbs switching on!

Are you an active participant in your own rescue or are you frozen with fear and still in the grip of your own crisis? If your home went up in flames what would you do? Would you crawl under the bed or would you become an active participant in your own rescue? For me, Ireland has not been an active participant in its own rescue. Sure, we have put our hands in our pockets and dug deep to bail out banks and, yes, we have done it with conviction and grace and dignity, but that was on the assumption that if we took the austerity we'd see inevitable improvement relatively quickly. However, that hasn't been the case, and yet we have not objected. We were sold a dud and we haven't reacted. Having said all that, I have first-hand experience of paying dearly for bad advice from some of the top accountants in the country. I, like many others, thought that a solicitor or an accountant was the first port of call for help with my finances and trusted that, because of the reputation and cost of the providers of this advice, what I received would be reliable, informed and helpful. That was not the case. It turns out I am not alone in this experience, and I suspect that many of the solicitors and accountants to whom people turn in times of financial turmoil might be experiencing some financial pressure themselves. But when the professionals don't know what to advise or how to help, people are left with nowhere else to go.

If you google business advice or help, you are presented with choices such as large accounting houses and/or business coaches who tend to be celebrity business people who (with respect) don't understand what it's like for an SME in rural Ireland during this economic crisis. So what do you do? Who can help and who will give you some credibility with the bank to make them interested in listening to you? This is a question I was frequently asked on my travels around the country. I felt very lucky that my recovery plan was working and I really wanted to be able to pass on to others what I had learned, but I didn't know how to do it. I referred people to ACT or described the work they did where I could. I read the book

The Secret in the midst of my own crisis and the two major things I took from it were positive thinking and gratitude. Having both was very important to me and by 2012 I felt both in abundance. That's why I felt compelled to spread the message that we should be active participants in our own rescue, and supply information about the steps that might be taken to facilitate that. That's why I set up Insight – to provide the option of getting advice from somebody who isn't famous, who has experienced the difficulties specific to a self-employed person in the SME sector in Ireland.

The implementation of a recovery plan is different in the context of your participation in your own rescue – you will not be enabled, you have to learn to do it yourself. Each of us needs to take stock of where we are and what needs to be done to start the rehabilitation of the business. It is also critical to create a strategy for the future based on income, household budget, educational and retirement requirements. Don't just live for today. Plan ahead now. Plan as though you'll live forever and live as though you'll die tomorrow. You must plan and then you must act. Failure to act on debt or negative equity within a certain time frame could limit your ability to recover. A lack of long-term thinking has given rise to problems for so many people and this must be avoided for future growth. Take the following as a case study of the consequences of not thinking for the long term:

A couple own a house they purchased four years ago with an interest-only mortgage of €800,000. The value of that property is now, say, €350,000. They each brought a property to the marriage (owned individually before they met), with no mortgage on either; however, as each property was either a townhouse or an apartment, they had a limited value. As well as the expensive family home, they bought one more investment property together, borrowing €275,000 on a 100 per cent mortgage in 2007, cross-charging that mortgage over the other three combined properties they owned. That property is now valued at €185,000. The couple are now both aged forty-nine with total borrowings including mortgages, personal loans and credit card bills of €1.175 million. They are servicing all of their debts on an interest-only basis but all payments are up to date and so the couple think they are doing fine – which they are, given the level of debt they are in. However, a closer examination of the household budget and their income excluding rental income (because that could disappear at any point pending market conditions) confirms that the couple can really only afford an interest and capital loan to the value of €285,000. They are depending on rental income, which can be fickle, and if it were to dry up they would struggle to make even the interest payments. At forty-nine years of age there are only around sixteen years to normal retirement and they still have not started making capital repayments on the mortgage for the private dwelling – some €800,000. There is no pension in place, they own property valued at €585,000 between their townhouse, apartment and the investment house they purchased together but, excluding the family home (as it would be expected that one would not sell the family home to liquidate assets in order to repay the bank), they have exposure to the banks on property alone of €1.075 million. So even if they could sell the apartment, townhouse and investment house to reduce their exposure, which is a big ask in this market, they would still be left with exposure to the bank of €490,000 with the capacity to repay only €285,000 and only sixteen years until retirement.

This couple will struggle hugely over the next decade and may face having to sell the family home because they didn't think long term and thought they were doing fine because they were making all of their interest-only repayments. But what if the bank changed the terms of the loan, forcing them to also start making capital repayments? Rental income is taxable and, if mortgage interest relief was cut or removed, they would face bigger cash-flow issues. As things stand they are being neither proactive nor reactive. By not taking the long-term view, they possibly don't even realise that they have a problem and they are certainly not active in bringing about a conclusion that will see them safely into retirement. They are doing nothing and they will pay the price for that down the line.

I fear that a great many people in Ireland are in a very similar situation. So far, this couple will not have been flagged by the banks as being a problem case, but they will be in the future, so the lack of action by banks and government on negative equity/ property value and/or debt resolution, combined with lack of understanding or action by borrowers, will do nothing but drag out the country's recession for another few years and slow down recovery on a national scale. It's a disaster. As a country we could wind up limping from arrears crisis to arrears crisis and who will end up paying for each crisis? Do we have a collective responsibility to act to prevent that situation in the future? Holding on to property only makes sense if capital and interest repayments can be sustained or if the possibility that property values might increase becomes imminent – and even at that, it would need to happen at a double-digit increase.

In the case of this unfortunate couple, there is something they can do now to stem the problem in the future. They can engage with their bank and demonstrate that potential financial difficulties are camouflaged within the portfolio. This will be more transparent if they present a detailed statement of affairs signed off by an accountant as well as a sworn affidavit to the effect that there are no other assets. A bank will not ignore such a level of preparation and detail. This will effectively confirm that if all the properties were offloaded, the couple could only afford a mortgage of €285,000. The couple could then formally apply for the following:

1. Permission to dispose of all properties except the family home at prices agreed by the bank.
2. The selling prices would reflect current property values.
3. All proceeds of the sales would go to the bank.
4. The fees payable to execute the property sales would be taken from the proceeds of the sales.
5. The home loan would be converted from interest-only to interest and capital repayments based on a loan value of €285,000 and any residual debt would be parked (not accumulating interest) for a period of, say, five years.

This would be massive progress for the couple and would reduce their debt on all fronts while keeping the family home safe. The only outstanding issue to be resolved would be the residual debt, which may ultimately form part of a long-term national banking strategy.

The desire to survive this crisis should not be based on pride. It must be based on the consequences of not surviving, and until we are truly faced with these consequences, many of us will fail to act. Failure to act, failure to consider the future, failure to comprehend the long-term implications of your financial position will certainly increase the rate of mortgage arrears, the rate of receiverships in business and possibly, then, the suicide rate in this country. I know that many Irish people continue to fail to address insolvency, hard-core personal debt and mortgage arrears and, in so doing, they remain blind to the horrific consequences that are lying in wait for them. Don't wait, move now and move at speed. Think long term. Think debt resolution. Seize the day because that option might not be around for long. Put your helmet on because there has never been a better time for a little white-water rafting.

Key Lesson: Be an active participant in your own rescue. It's the best advice that I got and will ever get during this or any crisis.

11

Family ties

Those whom we love most are often the most alien to us.

Christopher Paolini

Ours was a family business, and family businesses can bring with them complex problems that can impact the success and profitability of the business if not managed carefully. In *Shepherd's Pie* I described the fractious business relationship that I had with my father, which sometimes spilled over into our personal lives and affected other family relationships too. As ninety per cent of the indigenous business sector in Ireland is made up of family businesses, it is not surprising that I have been contacted not only by people who are struggling with a failing business, but also by many who are involved in family businesses that are doing all right or even quite well during the recession but have become battlegrounds for other reasons.[52] The complications that can arise in a family business can carry significant consequences for all concerned, very few of which may be positive. It is very difficult to discuss these issues openly and honestly and neutrally because, inevitably, emotions run

---

52 http://www.deloitte.com/view/en_IE/ie/news/ie-pressreleases-en/f51c98 7229bd0310VgnVCM3000001c56f00aRCRD.htm

high and feelings are hurt and that clouds objectivity and commercial reality. This kind of maelstrom can cause real pain and damage in both the family and the business. As I had talked about my family and our business, there was an interest from people wanting to know how everything had worked out between my father and me. One person said they thought that the family part of the story had ended on a note of 'To be continued ...'

My family were so brave to allow me to tell our story. We all knew that with the publication would come some local media attention (none of us bargained on the national attention it received) and I was worried about that for my parents especially. What would our friends and neighbours think and how would they react, not to me but to members of my family? Fortunately, any feedback they received was supportive and encouraging, and if there were any naysayers, they were respectful enough of my parents not to comment. Before the story was published I had given it to my immediate family to read. While my brother, sisters and Anne's parents were all supportive, sent best wishes for a job well done and ultimately gave it their blessing, there was plenty of discussion about how the disagreements and upset between my father and me had been conveyed. There were differing opinions, but my view was that in relating this story I had a responsibility to show respect for my parents, which I hope I did.

My father's review of the book was always going to be incredibly important to me and the last thing I wanted was to further complicate our relationship. The day I gave him the manuscript he was very eager to start reading it and, once he started, he kept disappearing to read it at every possible opportunity. He finished it in a couple of days and then he rang me to say that he thought it was a wonderful achievement and that he had loved reading it and would change nothing. He was so enthusiastic with his support. I was very touched by it and that night, when I went to bed, I wondered if the book had addressed some of the issues between us that we hadn't confronted face to face. I wondered what had gone through his mind when he had read some of the things I had written about and recalled those episodes. Whatever it was, we didn't discuss it in detail. There was no mention of specifics, but maybe reading the book had been as therapeutic for him as writing it had been for me. I hope that the long hard battles fought with my old man over the years are now behind us. I think they are.

We are so similar. Dad might not agree, but I believe that we share the same commercial instinct even though he takes a conservative approach and I am more bullish – although not so much recently! He is more of a people person than I am and, as a result, he always had a good relationship with his staff, where I struggled. He still commands significant local respect, whereas the jury is still out on me. I am spiritual but he is deeply religious. We were both rubbish at school. We are both workaholics. We both love business. In hindsight, had either one of us been able to take the emotion out of our business relationship and manage our egos, we could have made a fantastic team and avoided the collapse of the business – but then we might not have ended up with the innovative new business model either, so I try not to get stuck in the mindset of 'what if', and make the most of the relationship we have now.

I attended an event at which I was speaking in late 2011 and because so many people who I had met on my travels had asked how things were between the old man and myself, I invited him along to meet some of them. What a reaction! If I had brought Brad Pitt with me he wouldn't have had the same reaction. One member of the audience put their hand up to ask a question: 'I am delighted to see your father here with you this evening. Does that mean that things are now better between you?' I answered, 'We are both in therapy at the moment and it was suggested that it might be a good idea to spend some time together.' That got a big laugh from the audience. Dad was proud as punch. He was a big hit and I enjoyed having him there. The answer to the question on how things are between us is that yes, our relationship is much better. It is harmonious for the most part and that's not just because of my writing a book. For all the strife and hurt feelings that came with being part of a family business we have both come through it in one piece. I certainly have regrets and maybe he does too, I don't know, but things are good between us now.

I now see my parents daily. Both of them enjoy good health and both have settled into retirement better, knowing the business will survive. I suspect that the improvement in my relationship with my father must be a relief to my mother too. When the financial crisis and the ensuing collapse of the business came upon us, it distracted us from our battles. I think that at that stage, because Dad was pretty much gone from the business then, his paternal instinct kicked in as he witnessed my physical and emotional decline. He was worried about me. He watched as I came around to the emotional correction that kick-started my recovery and helped me fight back, and I think that was the point where our relationship changed for the better. I began to slowly pick up the pieces of the mess that had been left of the business he had started and I had grown, which had collapsed so dramatically. He saw my drive and determination not to give up and I think he respected that. I was always convinced that he didn't think I had what it takes to run a successful business, and that the collapse which had happened on my watch had served to confirm his opinion. But if that were the case, my response to the collapse, albeit not immediate, changed that.

The collapse of the business removed any possibility of any dividend for my parents, so aside from the fact that the business was no longer viable as it was, we had nothing more to disagree about. Dad's forced retirement (which is still a great regret of mine) left a bad smell for many years, but that's a moot point at this stage so we have moved on. He now views the company as being Brian's and mine. He recognises that it will take us years to rebuild, but I know that he now trusts me to run it because he has said so. No doubts. That's a massive change.

Retirement is a huge life change for anyone, especially for a person who was an active and driving force in their own business for many years, but Dad now accepts and is comfortable with retirement. He has never demonstrated any resentment for the damage caused to the business or the loss of any potential income for him as a result of the collapse, which I think is a measure of his character. For that I am hugely grateful and I have great respect for the man.

Now and then I feel quite emotional when I reflect on

the years we spent at loggerheads. My office overlooks the banks of the River Suir and my father walks the riverbank early every morning. I don't know how I know when to do it, but something always tells me when to look out the window. I raise my head and there he is looking up towards my office. He waves warmly, as I do in response. At that moment I know for certain that the wave is for his son and not the businessman. My wave is to my dad, now in his seventies. He turns and continues his walk. I wonder what he thinks, right at that moment. I wonder if his thoughts are similar to mine – that moments like this won't last forever.

Key Lesson: Avoid working with family if at all possible and, if you must, be very clear on roles, boundaries, responsibilities and expectations. Have patience, be objective and stick to the facts, removing emotion when making commercial decisions – if you can't, use the services of someone who can. Your family is too precious to risk.

12

Anne

Happiness is like a butterfly. The more you chase it, the more it eludes you. But if you turn your attention to other things, it comes and sits softly on your shoulder.

Henry David Thoreau

For better or for worse, for richer, for poorer, in sickness and in health. I think 'solvent or insolvent, within or without family business' should be added. Through my work at Insight I have met the husbands, wives and partners of so many self-employed people and two things are consistently high on their agendas. They want an end to the miserable existence that has gripped their families and their relationships as a result of either a failed business or property investments, and they fear greatly for their partners' mental and physical health. I see the strain they are under and the desperate hopelessness and helplessness they feel. I have been guilty of not recognising the pain I caused my wife at one point and I believe that it is incumbent on a person in a loving relationship to do everything in their power not to knowingly cause such pain to their partner.

I finally recognised the pain and stress I was causing my wife the day I told her that I would do whatever I had to do to return our lives to some kind of normality and harmony. I asked Anne to be patient and to give me time to get things back on track. She gave me her blessing to go and do whatever it was that I needed to do to regain a balance in our lives. That was in 2009 and I might as well have left home for two and a half years, because it took that length of time to get it done, although the knowledge that it was getting done certainly helped us to get by in the interim. I was there, at home, physically, but I was constantly distracted or working on some document for the bank or making plans for the business, so running our household and family and all that goes with it rested with Anne, who was also trying to cope with a fifty per cent decline in the turnover of her own boutique business and to ensure that it too survived. Her support that day and her decision to let me off for as long as I needed to sort out everything with the business was wise, insightful, selfless and brave. It was fifteen months into the collapse and we were both weary, fatigued and suffering emotionally, which had an inevitable impact on our relationship. It was six years after I had decided to expand the business and build the new showrooms. I had dedicated every working hour in the week to building what I thought would be our future, but it now seemed like it had all been for nothing. That day marked the start of our personal recovery too, not just from the collapse of the business and the economy, but from the years of disruption caused to our lives by the conflict between my father and me. It was a defining moment in our marriage.

I think that nine times out of ten, men, especially Irish men, keep their partners in the dark about their business problems. For some it's because they see the business of providing for the family as their domain and don't want to worry their partner with it, while others keep it to themselves or actively lie about any problems to save face or to avoid getting a kick in the balls. For whatever reason, too many men carry the strain alone. My advice would be: don't underestimate the power of sharing a problem. I have met too many widows who have lost their husbands to suicide and who were unaware of the depth of the crisis and anguish that their husbands were facing. Women are better at seeking support from their partners or other loved ones and so I believe they are less likely to suffer in silence and spiral into despair for business reasons – I have no proof of that but my experience of women's coping skills both in business and privately is a strong indicator. Personal and business recovery comes in different forms, but having listened to countless horror stories, I know that if either you or your business is in trouble it is vitally important that you communicate with your partner and explain what's going on with you openly and honestly – not only in business but in the relationship too, and how both are affecting you and your ability to cope. There may be shock, there may be tears and raised voices, but it will pass, and when it does you can both start to rebuild your life together and repair any damage that has been done to the relationship.

In my opinion and experience, approaching your rehabilitation as a couple, together, will give you a better chance of survival, and for some it could very well be the difference between life and death. You must come clean. You must face the music and tell your partner everything – it's never too late. Otherwise your relationship is doomed. However, I would also caution against overkill. Some business people burden their partners with their self-pity, which only serves to heighten fear and is hugely unproductive. I was like that at one point too and it's really damaging. It's irritating for your partner to listen to daily moaning and groaning, without you taking any action to help yourself or figure it out. There is a balance to be struck and for me it was ultimately about describing how I felt, explaining what I thought I needed to do and how long it would take, and what the consequences might be, both the positive and the negative. Striking this balance is critical for the survival of many stressed-out marriages – and I think that for most men the survival of their marriage is a key component of their coping ability.

Years ago, a close friend who was considering marriage asked me, how do you know if she is the right one for you? The answer I gave him at that point was hypothetical and little did I know how prophetic my own words would turn out to be for my own marriage. I told him to ask himself, is she somebody you can come home to some evening when you have really made a mess of things? I mean, really fucked up. Can you put your head in her lap and cry, knowing that she will not only comfort you but then help and advise you? If you believe she will support you in your darkest hour, then she's a keeper. Years later, my wife held my head in her hands as I sobbed uncontrollably during the peak of our crisis. Stress, fatigue, a sense of failure and financial ruin were bad enough, but thinking that I had failed Anne was unbearable and I was crumbling. Yet she was there to help, to rationalise, to encourage and reassure. Her love and support helped to protect my self-esteem, and without that my own personal recovery and emotional correction might never have got out of the starting blocks.

Having Anne in my life has made the difference for me – the difference between winning or losing the fight to survive on all fronts in my life. Anne and I celebrate our twenty-seventh year together in 2012. I can hardly believe it. I have a daughter who is sixteen, the age Anne was when we first met. Little did either set of parents know how in love we were as kids, but we both did. We knew it was forever. I still know it. Nothing has changed. I count myself lucky that despite the many difficulties we have had along the way, both as a result of being so involved in a family business and because of the collapse of the business in the recession, Anne and I have come out the other side much stronger as a couple. I don't think that a relationship can be tested to the extent that ours was and survive, without it having a positive impact. In our case, after we came through the tough times, I took our story public with the book and, again, Anne was supportive throughout. She has coped very well with the fact that the general public now knows so much about our journey, given how private a person she is. I know that deep down she would prefer that people didn't know so much, but she hasn't said so. I admire her bravery for allowing me to do what I did. I am blessed to have a partner who supports me in good times and in bad, and who understood what I needed from her when the chips were down. We went into crisis mode in early 2008 as a result of my business decisions and mine alone, many of which Anne didn't support from day one, so when those actions resulted in our life falling apart, it was mind-blowingly difficult for me to come clean, but she was so gracious and forgiving. My looking into her eyes at that point, seeking both forgiveness and help, defined our relationship and tested the vows we had taken when we were so young. In a magnificent display of strength, support and love, Anne responded brilliantly.

Key Lesson: Don't underestimate the powerful effect that this crisis is having on your long-term relationship. Ensure that your line of communication is open and proactive and that you are not just dumping your daily woes on your partner. Inform, yes. Moan, no. Communicate the action you need to take and the possible outcomes. Go into this battle together, both fully briefed. No surprises. No lies in the interest of protecting your partner. The problems must be shared. That's half the battle.

13

Plan B

When all else fails, fresh tactics!

John Travolta's character in the movie Face-Off

In 2004 I had a plan, let's call it Plan A. It was based on the facts I had before me at that time and was an expansion plan – I didn't plan for failure and didn't even entertain Plan B. That was an expensive mistake. Plan A was to transform our family business into a motor group, but it ultimately failed, despite having gotten off to a flying start, perhaps inevitably given what happened back in 2008 and how that continues to affect Ireland in particular. When I was looking online for descriptions of what happened, I found many references to the 'global financial collapse'. It has been described as 'the worst financial crisis since the Great Depression' of the 1930s and as having played a significant role in the failure of key businesses.[53] Nothing could have prepared anyone for this type of event. That's why I believe that everyone deserves a second chance, and if a second chance is given to those who need one, the knock-on effects will be felt throughout the economy and benefit all sectors of Irish society. But whether

---

53   http://online.wsj.com/article/SB122169431617549947.html

or not the success or failure of Plan A was beyond my control, it failed and I have to deal with the consequences and get on with things now. It's time to pick up the pieces and move on to Plan B. This time I will ensure I also have Plan C, just in case.

My Plan B came about when I started to become an active participant in my own rescue. Accepting what happened, accepting the consequences, accepting that I wanted to start again and that I was ready and willing to do so. That was the real turning point, when I dumped my self-pity and stopped waiting for an imaginary recovery in the economy, stopped hoping that the banks would quietly back off, understood that Plan A was over and that there was no way that it could be saved. When I stopped waiting for others, like the banks or the government or the EU, to solve my problems. When I stopped focusing on failure and let go of my anger and denial and stopped giving a shite about what anyone would think if I had to cease trading or sell a premises. It was a call to action by George Mordaunt for George Mordaunt. I was going to step up and create my own recovery.

But I was still at a loss about where to turn for guidance. I didn't know who could help or who would really know what to do. It certainly wasn't any of the accountants or solicitors that I had hired over the years. I trawled websites, sent emails to forums seeking advice or a recommendation for a consultant, bought books, newspapers, business magazines, and put in hours of research that yielded nothing – no advice, no assistance for someone who simply doesn't know where to start. The reason for that is simple – there is nobody that I could find who can advise you on how to start your individual recovery, meeting your own needs in a practical way. There isn't a website that you can go to or a support group or a counsellor that specialises in a self-employed person's recovery from a global financial crisis. So many people were left shell-shocked, just like I was, with no idea where to turn. The irony is that there are support groups for many of the consequences of this crisis, such as divorce, stroke, depression, eating disorders, bullying and suicide bereavement, but no support to get to recovery, where those consequences can be avoided. Instead, we have layers of bureaucracy, retrospective regulation, finger-pointing, blame and recrimination, whereas I believe we should have business clinics that focus on coping with the collapse of a business and therefore a livelihood when there is no entitlement to social welfare as a self-employed person. Or some kind of service that helps and advises people who either continue to struggle or are having difficulty coping, picking up the pieces, moving on, forming Plan B. No such service existed when this all started in 2008 and I desperately needed somewhere to turn. Five years later, there is still no such impartial, free service. In a way, this is what this chapter is trying to address. Plan B can be our Chapter 11 in Ireland. It can be our second chance. It might start someone on the road to recovery.

I came across the following beautiful paragraph from a woman who had suffered with anorexia for many years. Evidently, she chose to become an active participant in her own recovery and wrote about it in a way that reminds me of what's happening across the SME sector in Ireland at the moment. When I read this I substitute the words 'eating disorder activist' with businessperson and 'anorexia' with fear, but it is relevant and applicable to all sorts of recovery from all sorts of situations:

A recovered life is all about living a fulfilling authentic life, despite its obstacles. I am an eating disorder activist who believes in FULL recovery. Why? Because I consider myself proof. After too many years of anorexia and depression I have turned my life around and am living a life I never knew was possible. I want to help others to do this.[54]

Any of the steps that I took between March 2008 and March 2012 to deal with the collapse of the family business, the huge pressure from banks to deal with debt, which affected my mental and physical health, my emotional correction, the recovery of the business and the return to something that resembles a normal life, were not premeditated, but rather were the consequences of events that were taking place at the time. Some of the steps were a reaction to events that were outside my control, but some were part of a strategy that was agreed on as events unfolded. In this chapter, I want to summarise those steps in the hope that having it all listed in one place might be useful, and that there may be something in my experience that can help someone else. I took all of these steps, but I stress that the decisions I made were based on my own experiences and not on any qualification or education other than my very real experience in an SME in rural Ireland. They might not suit everybody, but might provide guidance or food for thought to anyone whose circumstances resemble mine, because they were the fundamental steps that drove my recovery.

---

54 http://eatingdisorderrecovery.tumblr.com/post/16374513015/a-recovered-life-love-this

Decide that you will no longer suffer from the disease to please

No more thinking, planning or behaving in a manner that pleases banks, institutions, employees or anyone else who is making demands on you. Express yourself and call it as it is. If you're broke, you're broke. So what? Don't pretend. Don't lie. Open and frank discussions are needed more than ever. Most people or businesses in your sector will be able to relate and you never know what you will get back. In November 2010 I did exactly that when I stood in front of 200 business owners, customers, government ministers, bankers and members of my family and told them 'I've fucked up and now I'm broke.'

Seek advice

It might be difficult to identify who the right person or organisation is, but it's important to find someone to talk to about both your practical and emotional needs. Compile relevant and accurate information about your business and personal finances. Stick to the facts. Follow the money. Make a decision about your next steps when you have exhausted all of your questions and possible outcomes. Be brave and remember creativity, planning and research, decisiveness. Seeking advice from ACT was one of the most important steps that I took. Theirs is a service that helps people to help themselves – think of retaining a service such as that as additional management capacity in your business.

Educate yourself

Know your rights. Read and understand the Consumer Codes of Protection. Nothing remains the same in the banking sector as a result of the global financial collapse, so educate yourself on how to communicate with banks post-bailout.

Review all your paperwork and then approach the bank

I mean everything. All legal and financial documents that you have signed. Everything relating to anything you have as security on a loan, every sanction letter, every interest rate change. Look for inconsistency. Up to 2009 the paper trail from the banks was pretty sloppy. Look for any angle that allows you to question them. Compile a timeline of your correspondence with them, documenting any changes or inconsistencies you find. Do not accept an increase in your interest rate because of 'your credit profile'. Ensure you separate your personal finances from investment property and from your commercial entity.[55] Ensure you have a copy of every document you should have from the bank and order a copy if you don't have it. Do not be dictated to by banks. You did a deal, you had an agreement and it was that you got their money while they got your security. Give it to them. Resist the urge to increase the value of your security. Don't give the bank more security. Don't cross charge. Under no circumstances should you give personal guarantees. Once you

---

55 To do this you will need to compile: a) a statement of affairs for all in-come excluding salary and including details of all loans and interest repay-ments together with asset values and a detailed household budget. Use the one in the Appendix as a guide; b) Management accounts with full details of the performance of your company. Both documents should be compiled separately but each one is applicable and relevant to the overall solution to the debt prob-lem. The performance of the company demonstrates future potential earnings and repayment capacity on commercial debt, which will impact the household budget and therefore disposable income. Disposable income will dictate the repayment capacity on personal debt.

have scrutinised everything and know exactly where you stand, make an approach and work with the bank, without allowing them to intimidate you – they can't intimidate you unless you allow them to. It's their problem too, but it's up to you to be proactive and offer a solution. I offered to play an active role in selling my property, keeping control of the portfolio to ensure I avoided a receivership, which in turn avoided a fire sale and reduced the amount I owed as well as saving the bank the cost of a receiver. Your objective is to end the misery, so put everything on the table, demonstrate your knowledge, how prepared you are and how committed you are to the process of resolving your problems. Don't commit to anything you are not sure you can do and deliver on everything you commit to. Don't ask naive questions about debt forgiveness – look at this issue from the perspective of the bank and ensure that they see you as a credible candidate for a possible joint resolution to your debt problem. Understanding that could be the key to your future; failure to grasp it could be disastrous. Make sure you have a ticket IF the debt forgiveness train pulls into the station. Be completely transparent and ensure you are meticulously prepared for any meetings with the bank with all of the correct documentation, and take plenty of notes at your meetings.

It's time to end the standoff between the Irish business community and its banking sector. We must not let Irish banks control either our economy or our society. For those who are still in fear of the banks, please don't be frightened. Engage with them transparently and don't accept intimidation. If that requires you to put pen to paper to inform senior officials that the way the bank is communicating with you is intimidating you, then do so. Banks now have to abide by a code of conduct introduced by the financial regulator and if they are not behaving according to that code, force them to.

Go for Plan B

You deserve a second chance. Ireland needs entrepreneurs – they will be the real drivers of the economy over the next ten years. The fact that many self-employed people whose businesses went bust are prepared to start again shows grit and a determination not to give up, to create employment and to contribute to the recovery of the local economy. We have learned the hard lessons. Evoke your own Chapter 11 and be ready with your Plan B. Don't be afraid. Plan it, prepare for it and do it. This course of action may be ruthless, but if you are self-employed and your business fails, you don't qualify for social welfare, so how will you put food on the table? If failure of a business is inevitable, you have no choice. You might have to cease trading on a Friday and begin again with a new company the following Monday. Ruthless undoubtedly, but it might be your only chance and it's all about your survival.

Deal with debt on commercial and/or residential investment property

Negative equity on anything but the family home must be offloaded. It will be more than ten years before property values return to a level where negative equity is a thing of the past. Don't waste time and money thinking that you are sitting pretty servicing interest-only mortgages. For most people now, property is just like a toxic bank share – you have to dump it. It will sell at today's rock bottom prices. To do this you need to justify to the bank why it needs to go. You must fully and clearly demonstrate that you can no longer afford the property. Work with the bank again. Avoid a rent receiver.[56] A bank allowed me to retain seventeen per cent of my gross rental income to manage my own property portfolio for things like insurance, household charge, etc. It was either allow me the ability to pay the standard property charges or pay a receiver much more to do the same thing. All sorts of deals are being done, for example, having an expiry date on a judgement rather than a lifelong threat, which I believe is an acceptable exit strategy from negative equity – but I think that there will be no hope of anything that resembles debt resolution for those who continue to retain ownership of property.

Ask the hard questions

Before you decide to continue in business as a self-employed person, ask yourself, is this what you want and where you want to be? If it is, can you create or stimulate new business? Will this business improve your quality of life? What about family life and your health? What is the right thing to do? If you could walk into your office every morning with no debt following, would you walk in with a spring in your step? Or do you have a genuine desire to start again, doing something different or in a new business? It's brutal out there in Irish business and it will be for some time to come. By all accounts there is no immediate economic recovery on the horizon,

---

56 A rent receiver is authorised to collect rental income from an investment property on behalf of a lending institution where loan repayments are not being made.

which means that many will continue to struggle and that in turn will affect your business. Your own mental and physical health and your family must come first. Maybe the more mature and considered approach is to move away from being self-employed.

Don't moan

If you decide to remain working for yourself having asked the hard questions, get on with it and practise positive thinking. Don't continue to assume that the lack of business is solely as a result of recession. It isn't. There are businesses that are doing very well. Assuming you have already cut all the fat, concentrate on moving forward and creating new business. There is an economy out there. The world still turns and technology has exploded since the beginning of the global financial crisis. Businesses that are performing well have engaged with technology to sell and market their products and services. The next generation is coming and they will only ever have known a world of touch screens and online shopping.

Create, research, decide

The quickest route to recovery is to stimulate sales. You must get more customers interested in your business so that you have more sales leads and close more sales. To do this you will have to be creative. You must engage with digital technology to do business and you must try to stand out from your competition. There is absolutely no room for complacency. You have probably been distracted from the core of the business for a few years, trying to sort out the mess, but you must get back to the heart of it. Try adding something to your business that you think might generate more revenue. This is your second chance. Think of it as a start up – be lean and be bold.

I think that the economic crisis in Ireland is evolving all the time and we didn't understand the depth of it or its potential to also damage our society so badly when it began. Our infamous bank guarantee was given without accurate or truthful information on the night. The mess was so big that the banks themselves had to grapple with how to address the problem and went running to the elected government of the people they are now grinding down. Their dogged pursuit of the recovery of impossible loans has resulted in a level of fear and low morale that has halted any sign of a return of consumer confidence that could drive the economy. However, there are changes afoot in the banking sector and that's good news. I believe that five years from now the banking sector will be totally different, and who knows, maybe the banks will have learned something. I have certainly learned from this experience. I have learned that to recover, I needed to separate the topic from the issue. This is not just semantics, there is a fundamental difference between the two things. The topic is your debt, the bank, sales/your business. The issue is you. It's your failure to act, to resolve, to create, to conclude, to sell, to propose, to self-educate, to engage, to become an active participant in your rescue.

There is a future for indigenous business in Ireland but business has to change, discover new models and stay lean. The day I wrote this chapter, I had four cars due in from the UK in the morning, all pre-sold. We had two to buy that same morning and had three already purchased but not paid for, waiting for collection. We had delivered four more to their new owners the day before. In the last five working days we had recorded over 160 enquiries for cars by email, phone and people walking in. We had refused four deals in the previous week because the margin would not have met our profitability criteria – we set targets based on margin now, not volume. This happened in what is usually considered to be the second quietest month in the motor industry. Those enquiries were not generated from a showroom located in the heart of one of Ireland's major cities. They all came from Clonmel (population circa 20,000) in the middle of arguably the deepest recession since the foundation of the State. I think that shows promise. We could do with hiring more staff, but we will resist for now. We need to be sure that the business they bring in will pay for their keep. We will soon launch a new website that will be our best salesperson and will offer a better and more unique experience to our customers. Our bank accounts are always in credit – we don't have an overdraft facility by choice and therefore have no interest charges. We don't borrow. We pass the fees for paying by credit card on to our customers because we cannot absorb that without eroding our margin, and we also charge an administration fee. We state the administration fee up front and it's non-negotiable, and then we state the price separately so that the customer can clearly see the breakdown. We sell warranties for cars but we don't do the unprofitable warranty and service work ourselves. We don't do anything for free any more, but we do offer an exceptionally competitive price and we deliver on quality. We provide a very detailed personal service. It is the exact opposite of what we were doing five years ago. It works really well for both us and our customers and, dare I say it, work has become enjoyable and satisfying again.

I'm sharing this to demonstrate that recovery is possible if you choose it, if you separate the topic and the issue and decide to address the issue. Don't ignore what is happening in the Irish banking sector, economy or society and thereby stall your recovery. Be alert, stay informed and keep pace with your market. Recovering and rebuilding a healthy business is possible in Ireland – it is certainly not an easy task and will have tough challenges, but they are not insurmountable. Having been to hell and back in business in this country since 2008, I can say that with certainty.

Key Lesson: Try and fail but don't fail to try.

14

Half-time whistle

The secret of a rich life is to have more beginnings than endings.

Dave Weinbaum

On a Monday in 2012 I joined my parents and my brother Brian for a quiet lunch in Clonmel, to mark the thirtieth anniversary of the Mordaunt family in the Irish motor industry. During the meal, we reflected on our collective experience of the business, which had exposed us to all sorts of emotions as a family. Together we had experienced success and failure, growth and contraction, wealth and an extreme cash famine. At its best, the business had created a very comfortable lifestyle for the entire family, giving all of us a great start in life. At its worst, it had divided us in a most acrimonious way, which has certainly left scars. Not every family member was directly involved in the business but every family member was directly affected by it in terms of income, relationships with each other and succession. Rightly or wrongly, I began to feel like the company I was working my ass off to grow and then to save was nothing more than a gravy train for everyone else. For ten long years we argued in offices, kitchens, forecourts and living rooms, and during those battles we got everything said and expressed every emotion. We eventually found a balance between the family business and the family, but it was hard fought for every one of us. It was a victory though, as each family member went through their own journey with the business and each one is thriving now that we have separated the business from the family, which would probably not have happened had the Irish economy not collapsed and our business with it. So the harmony in our family is another positive that has come out of the trials and tribulations of the last five years and will almost certainly make for a better family life for the next generation. So our quiet lunch marked what the business, and all that had happened to it, meant for each of us individually and as a family. We all knew that it was time to put the past behind us and look only to the future.

Returning to the office from the restaurant that afternoon, I passed the original forecourt on which my father had started the business. It lies idle now, owned by someone else. He had started the business in 1982 with £17,000 and one car. He had four young kids, a mortgage with an interest rate of seventeen per cent, it was the middle of a recession and he was forty-four years old. Between that date and 2002 when he left the business, he did very well and created a very comfortable retirement for himself. So when I was on the edge in 2010 he told me to get my head up and start again, and look at what I could start over with compared to what he had started with. I was also forty-four. I also had a huge mortgage but I was starting again with a brand that had thirty years of goodwill behind it, a premises, fifty cars, over 3,000 customers and twenty-five years experience in business. I could see his point! There were still enormous difficulties to overcome, but I knew that the most important thing was to ensure I could earn a living to support my family. Putting food on the table was my first priority and once that was done, the other battles I needed to fight could be addressed. If I could achieve half of what my father had achieved in the same time period, I would be fine. I set upon the notion that it was half-time in the game of my life. The whistle had just been blown on the first twenty-five years. I wasn't winning, I was losing, but it was against the run of play, so if at half-time I could pick myself up and dust myself down, I could go back out for the second half and turn it around, provided that I had the resolve and the mental and physical fitness. Before the whistle goes for the second half, I have set out some ground rules:

1. I will get one chance only to get back in front.
2. I cannot make the same mistakes I made in the first half.
3. I must control the play, play smart and lead.
4. I must play creatively.
5. There is no room for complacency on the field of play.

The first half was the lesson and the second half is the exam. I am definitely on the back foot after the first twenty-five years of my working life, but there is absolutely no way that I will ever be back where I was in 2010 again. Moving forward is the only option and there is no room for apathy or negativity. Ireland was hit by recession but talked itself into a depression. I don't understand why the country is so slow to pick itself up and move on. I don't understand why our lives are still dominated by banks, five years later. I cannot understand why we are so negative and wonder if we will ever change. Where is our resolve to recover and to succeed, to take our place among the nations of the world? Our begrudgery is toxic. Throwing in the towel is not an option for any of us as individuals, businesses or as a country. Behind every successful business there are many unsuccessful years. The same can be said for an economy. Our moaning and negativity has fuelled our downward spiral. I believe that if our behaviour and attitudes were more positive, if we were more supportive of each other in both business and society and tried to see the bigger picture in our attempt to turn negative opinion into positive or neutral comment, we might not have to resort to ruthless survival tactics and might by now have started a national recovery. This little fable and its attendant lesson illustrates what I mean:[57]

A group of frogs were hopping contentedly through the woods, going about their froggy business, when two of them fell into a deep pit. All of the other frogs gathered around the pit to see what could be done to help their companions. When they saw how deep the pit was, they agreed that it was hopeless and told the two frogs in the pit that they should prepare themselves for their fate, because they were as good as dead.

Unwilling to accept this terrible fate, the two frogs began to jump with all of their might. Some of the frogs shouted into the pit that it was hopeless, and that the two frogs wouldn't be in that situation if they had been more careful, more obedient to the froggy rules, and more responsible. The other frogs continued sorrowfully shouting that they should save their energy and give up, since they were already as good as dead.

---

57   http://www.crystal-reflections.com/stories/story_73.htm

The two frogs continued jumping with all their might, and, after several hours of this, were quite weary. Finally, one of the frogs took heed to the calls of his fellow frogs. Exhausted, he quietly resolved himself to his fate, lay down at the bottom of the pit, and died.

The other frog continued to jump as hard as he could, although his body was wracked with pain and he was quite exhausted. Once again, his companions began yelling for him to accept his fate, stop the pain and just die. The weary frog jumped harder and harder and, wonder of wonders, finally leaped so high that he sprang from the pit.

Amazed, the other frogs celebrated his freedom and then gathering around him asked, 'Why did you continue jumping when we told you it was impossible?'

The astonished frog explained to them that he was deaf, and as he saw their gestures and shouting, he thought they were cheering him on. What he had perceived as encouragement inspired him to try harder and to succeed against all odds.

This simple story contains a powerful lesson. The Book of Proverbs says, 'There is death and life in the power of the tongue'. Your encouraging words can lift someone up and help them make it through the day. Your destructive words can cause deep wounds; they may be the weapons that destroy someone's desire to continue trying – or even their life. Your destructive, careless words can diminish someone in the eyes of others, destroy their influence and have a lasting impact on the way others respond to them. Be careful what you say.

Speak life to, and about, those who cross your path.

There is enormous power in words. If you have words of kindness, praise or encouragement, speak them now to, and about, others. Listen to your heart and respond. Someone, somewhere, is waiting for your words …

I believe that mentality needs to become an everyday feature for Irish business. Our media seems to be obsessed with reporting on IBRC, banks annual reports, NAMA, the HSE and the budget for six months before and three months after its publication. This constant hammering home of the negatives that are definitely present in our society and economy but not where our focus should be, is doing nothing to encourage positivity or hope. The world is rapidly changing and our country is transforming before our very eyes. If someone had walked up to you on Saint Patrick's Day 2008 and said that by the time we reached the same day in 2013, the British queen would not just have visited Ireland but would be so welcomed by the Irish people that she would travel to Northern Ireland and shake hands with Martin McGuinness, you would have said, 'Yeah right, and there goes a flying pig.' If that person had gone on to say that by 2012 Ireland would be losing over 1,000 people a week to emigration, that Fianna Fáil would be decimated in an election and reduced to just twenty seats, that the Irish taxpayer would own Permanent TSB, AIB and part of Bank of Ireland, that Anglo Irish Bank would no longer exist, having fleeced the taxpayer for millions to pay its bondholders, that the former chairman of Anglo would be facing trial, Seán Quinn would be bankrupt and then jailed, and some of Ireland's most tenacious entrepreneurs would be removed from business, a new Irish bank called NAMA would hold one of the world's largest property portfolios, Ireland would be halfway through a bailout programme having lost its sovereign financial governance, and that we would have come close to the failure of the European single currency at least three times, all to the backdrop of a baby boom,[58] as well as massive increases in suicide rates,[59] you would have backed away calmly and thought, 'What a nut job.' But if you were then told that the failed and bailed banks would be running the show, that you would be paying tax for water usage, that you could buy a full housing estate on several acres of land for about €150,000, that the properties that you thought would be your pension would be in negative equity and unsaleable, as well as being subject to three different taxes or charges, you would have called the men in white coats to remove this stark raving lunatic. No way could any of that ever happen, never mind in just five years, you might have thought. But it did and we haven't objected with any solidarity. I'm quite ashamed of how Ireland has reacted and conducted itself over the last few years, but I suppose time will tell if keeping our heads down and being teacher's pet in Europe will serve us well in the end.

And what about those Irish men and women who are well beyond the half-time whistle? How difficult is it for those whose pensions were their blue-chip bank shares? Many of them won't have the luxury of starting over and their financial plight will be ignored if they are retired. Should they be compensated? They placed their trust in highly paid bankers

---

58 http://www.irishtimes.com/newspaper/breaking/2012/0531/breaking27.html

59 http://www.irishcentral.com/news/Suicide-rate-rising-rapidly-in-Ireland-as-recession-grips-138771164.html

whose actions have wiped out share values and therefore the livelihoods of risk-averse investors. What can Ireland do for them? We cannot ignore them if we talk about debt resolution for mortgage holders or businesses, because they are as vulnerable as any other sector of society that has been side-swiped by an unprecedented and previously unimaginable global crisis that became a local one.

What will the next five years bring? How can we prepare as individuals or businesses and as a country? What will be required of us to succeed and how can we benefit from the inevitable changes? Recovery can and will present opportunities that heretofore have not been available or possible. We need to learn from the mistakes of our past and use the knowledge we have gained to secure our future. But we have to act, we have to make it happen. Neither the banks nor the government will create our second chance, only we can do that. Our future depends on the action we take today. We must plan for the future and see the bigger picture. Where do you want to be in ten years or at retirement? You need to lay the foundations for that plan now.

An elderly carpenter was ready to retire. He told his employer-contractor of his plans to leave the house-building business and live a more leisurely life with his wife enjoying his extended family. He would miss the pay cheque, but he needed to retire. They could get by.

The contractor was sorry to see his good worker go and asked if he could build just one more house as a personal favour. The carpenter said yes, but in time it was easy to see that his heart was not in his work. He resorted to shoddy workmanship and used inferior materials. It was an unfortunate way to end his career.

When the carpenter finished his work and the builder came to inspect the house, the contractor handed the front-door key to the carpenter. 'This is your house,' he said, 'my gift to you.'

What a shock! What a shame! If he had only known he was building his own house, he would have done it all so differently. Now he had to live in the home he had built none too well.

So it is with us. We build our lives in a distracted way, reacting rather than acting, willing to put up less than the best. At important points we do not give the job our best effort.

Then with a shock we look at the situation we have created and find that we are now living in the house we have built. If we had realized, we would have done it differently. Think of yourself as the carpenter. Think about your house. Each day you hammer a nail, place a board, or erect a wall. Build wisely. It is the only life you will ever build. Even if you live it for only one day more, that day deserves to be lived graciously and with dignity. The plaque on the wall says, 'Life is a do-it-yourself project.' Who could say it more clearly? Your life today is the result of your attitudes and choices in the past. Your life tomorrow will be the result of your attitudes and the choices you make today.[60]

Life is a do-it-yourself project. If you can live well and build

---

60   http://academictips.org/blogs/how-are-you-building-your-life/

something worth living for, you will gain an appreciation of what's important to you and what drives you to succeed, as well as the understanding that only you can live your life and you have the power to choose how you do that. Whatever you want to achieve in the future, you have to plan to achieve. The quoted story could demonstrate the state of the nation at the moment – Ireland is the contractor and its people are the carpenters. But it doesn't have to be like that. We can change it. I don't mean we should be rioting in the streets necessarily, but we can effect a change in attitude and exercise our democratic right to communicate with our politicians. We can do some research and really engage with the democratic process to decide for ourselves during the next referendum or election, and not just react to sensational broadcasting. The facts are there for us to examine if we bother to. We can demonstrate and protest peacefully yet, if in great enough numbers, powerfully. We can petition. We can strike, boycott, blockade and sit-in. The media can help. We can demonstrate that we do not accept the action that has been taken and has destroyed our lifestyle. If we expressed our disgust or dissatisfaction with how the country is being run with the same passion that we afford our under-achieving soccer team or put into going on the piss, then we may well have progressed beyond the situation that we are now in.

Ireland needs a comeback. I fear it is decades away because the carpenters are showing no sign of improving their shoddy work. Changing that will be the result of what we do tomorrow. What are you going to do tomorrow? What three or four things will you do to help make a change in your life to lay the foundations for your future? What contribution are you going to make to your recovery if that's your situation? Are you doing enough? If you got a second chance would you take it? History has shown us that human resolve can overcome global crises, financial meltdown, war, dictatorship and all sorts of natural disasters. Ireland is no different. We can overcome this crisis, and a good start would be changing our attitude and embracing the future and all it will bring, to encourage, self-educate and resolve to do whatever it takes to recover and to succeed.

Key Lesson: If you're lucky enough to get a second chance, don't cock it up. Learn from the mistakes of the past. Understand the power of an encouraging word. Think positively and don't allow negativity to dominate your thoughts or behaviour. Positive thinking is a habit and one that will stand you in good stead for the rest of your life, so it is a habit worth forming. Remember as often as you can that life is a do-it-yourself project, and do it.

Epilogue

I have had a wonderful opportunity to share a story about the journey taken by an Irish family business in a five year period, which is anything but unique. There is always a risk of a backlash when you say something that could be considered controversial or contrary to popular opinion, and I fully take that on board, but my family are exposed to whatever public reaction I get too and I am so grateful to them for allowing me to do it. I'm sure they will be relieved to know that, unlike when I downed tools after writing *Shepherd's Pie*, I feel that it's done now, this story has reached its natural conclusion. I don't have that same unsettled feeling. I am calmer. I thought I felt unsettled because I believed that we as a nation hadn't done enough to stand up for ourselves and take hold of our own recovery, but, in hindsight, I think really it was because I felt I hadn't done enough myself. This time, I know I've done everything I could do. My work in Insight and with ACT continues weekly. I still get many calls from people around the country seeking help or advice, and if I ultimately pass them on to ACT, Seán and Tommy seem to be able to weave their magic every time. Even though I hope that our combined efforts continue to help people turn their lives and businesses around for many years to come, part of me hopes the need for the service we provide will become less and less in the next five years.

So life goes on for all the gang at The Mordaunt Group. We

are recovering, making progress and achieving our business goals. Sales have improved and there are days when I think we need one or two new recruits, but so far I have resisted because I know I have to protect our margin. The old George Mordaunt would not have been so restrained – now I'll do the job myself. It will be some time before any substantial profits return, but we are thankful that at least we have stopped losing money. We are managing our costs and running a very lean business, but there is no more panic or stress. We are in calm waters now.

I think I can say that the decisions I have made so far to get to recovery have been the right ones, but we still review everything regularly and time will tell. The fear still creeps in often when I see the bank balance going scarily low, but I have learned to deal with my own fears and won't allow them and the negativity to control me ever again. Our showroom is busy and buzzing with footfall and enquiries. People have been so supportive, willing us to succeed and travelling from all over the country to offer us the chance of a deal so that they could help. There has been so much goodwill. This is quite a paradox for me because I feel and see this encouragement on a local level daily, but it seems to be lacking on a national scale – or maybe that's just how it's reported, I don't know. Our business model is very different to the usual dealership model and I truly believe that the day that decision was made was a turning point in our story. I fear for the Irish motor industry and what's still to come. I can't see anything on the horizon to indicate that a positive change is coming, and while I believe that the industry will survive, I fear for many of its captains. I thank God every day that we have removed ourselves from that market. The Mordaunt Group will soon celebrate its thirty-first year and I hope that, as with a fine wine, time will only make it better.

It will soon be exactly five years from the night when I celebrated my fortieth birthday in extravagant style, surrounded by my sixty staff and believing that it marked a milestone of success in my life, as I had achieved my dream of creating a motor group and being its head honcho. How deluded was I? Clearly I had no idea of what was really important and measured my success in a way that demonstrated that. If anyone had said to me that night that all of these people would lose their jobs, all of my showrooms bar one would close, I would resign all of my franchises, I would become an importer and sell cars nationally instead of locally, crucify myself emotionally and financially along the way, and tell my story in two books which would see me interviewed on TV and in newspapers, from *The New York Times* to *The Late Late Show*, I would have said WTF did you just smoke? It goes to show that no one knows what's next, what's around the corner or just over the horizon. That's the thrill of living in my view.

One dark and miserable winter's night four years ago, when I stood in my son's room watching him sleep peacefully and some survival instinct stirred in me, I hoped that, one day in the not-too-distant future, I would get home on a Friday evening after a long week's hard graft to sit with my family and watch a movie with a takeaway meal and a glass of wine, and that we would all then be able to sleep comfortably under our own roof. It seemed like bliss then and it still does now. It's called peace of mind and it is priceless. I will never compromise it again.

Despite enormous challenges, my family and our business are still standing, hand in hand, shoulder to shoulder, braced for the next challenge that is down the track. It will arrive, I have no doubt. What we have experienced and learned, not only in the last five years, but over the thirty years we have been in business, will stand to us. We know what's important and we know what we need to do to ensure not only our survival, but our success. I sincerely hope that sharing my story and experience of survival and recovery in an Irish family business in the aftermath of the global financial crisis has helped or will help someone who is struggling, or facing the prospect of losing everything they have worked for and having to make life-changing decisions. I wanted to end this story on a positive note and with a powerful message, and I found this saying, which I hope achieves just that: 'You know that life is worth the struggle when you look back on what you lost and realise what you have now is way better than before.'

Appendix

(REPRODUCED WITH KIND PERMISSION OF TOMMY MURPHY, ADVANCED CORPORATE TRANSFORMATIONS)

STATEMENT OF AFFAIRS
JACK & MARY

PREPARED BY: TOMMY MURPHY, ADVANCED CORPORATE TRANSFORMATIONS

NOVEMBER 2012

CONTENTS

STATEMENT OF AFFAIRS

| JACK & MARY | | November 2012 | | | PREPARED BY: TOMMY MURPHY, ADVANCED CORPORATE TRA |

No	Name of Property	Ownership	Asset Value	Loan Balance	Net Equity	Account Number	Ter
PERSONAL							
1	Private Home	Jack & Mary	240,000	275,000	(35,000)	AIB1162210	
2	Personal Loan - Credit Card	Jack & Mary	0	6,500	(6,500)		
3	Personal Current Account	Jack & Mary	0	9,153	(9,153)	MBNA	
						AIB 26111211	
	Personal Income	See Page 3					
	Personal Living Expenses	See Page 3					
	PERSONAL -TOTAL		240,000	290,653	(50,653)		
				121%	-21%		
INVESTMENT PORTFOLIO							
	Current Account	Jack & Mary		5,000	(5,000)	UB	
AIB							
1	20 Investment Lane	Jack & Mary	135,000	235,000	(100,000)	AIB300000	
2	21 Investment Lane	Jack & Mary	135,000	235,000	(100,000)	AIB300000	
AIB TOTAL			270,000	470,000	(200,000)		
				174%	-74%		
LESS PROPERTY COSTS							
NET RENTAL INCOME							
PTSB							
1	Dream Site	Jack & Mary	34,000	140,000	(106,000)	PTSB20000	
PTSB TOTAL			34,000	140,000	(106,000)		
				412%	-312%		
LESS PROPERTY COSTS							
NET RENTAL INCOME							
NET RENTAL INCOME -TOTAL			304,000	610,000	(306,000)		
				201%	-101%		
BUSINESS							
1	Overdraft			20,000	(20,000)		
2	Loan			0			
BUSINESS - TOTAL			0	20,000	(20,000)		
NET EQUITY - TOTAL			544,000	920,653	(376,653)		
				169%	-69%		
	PENSION FUND						
1	New Ireland	Jack	56,000		56,000	New Ireland	
2	ANO	Mary	0			ANO	
			56,000		56,000		

		CURRENT SITUATION			RESTRUCTURED SITUATION			
	Int Rate	Monthly Repayment	Monthly Income	Monthly Plus(Minus)	Monthly Repayment	Monthly Income	Monthly Plus(Minus)	STRATEGY
	Tracker 1.6%	367		(367)	367		(367)	Remain as is
		500		(500)	400		(400)	Reduce monthly repayment
	7.95%							
			4,797	4,797		4,797	4,797	
		4,026		(4,026)	4,026		(4,026)	
		4,893	4,797	(96)	4,793	4,797	4	
								To be used as Investment Account to track all rental, mortgages and costs.
	Tracker 2.1%	411	500	89	0	500	500	Agree to sell on a phased basis subject to bank approval and discontinue repayments
	Tracker 2.1%	411	500	89	411	500	89	Agree to sell on a phased basis subject to bank approval
		823	1,000	178	411	1,000	589	
				(506)			(506)	
				(329)			82	
	6.00%	700	0	(700)	0	0		Stop repayments and aggressively market the site for sale
		700	0	(700)	0	0		
				(42)			(42)	
				(742)			(42)	
				(1,071)			40	
		0	0	0	0	0	0	
				(1,167)			44	
		0		0	0		0	Frozen due to repayment incapacity
				0			0	
				0			0	

PROPERTY COSTS

| JACK & MARY | | | November 2012 | | PREPARED BY: TOMMY |

No	Name of Property	Rates	Household Charge	PRTB	Insuran
AIB					
1	20 Investment Lane	0	8	12	42
2	21 Investment Lane	0	8	0	42
		0	16	12	84
PTSB					
1	Dream Site	0	0	0	42
		0	0	0	42
GRAND-TOTAL MONTHLY		0	16	12	12
GRAND-TOTAL ANNUAL		0	196	144	1,5

ADVANCED CORPORATE TRANSFORMATIONS

f Fees	Management Fees	Maintenance	Mortgage Premiums	NPPR	TOTAL		ANNUAL
46	0	125	10	16	259		3,108
46	0	125	10	16	247		2,968
92	0	250	20	32	506		6,076
0	0	0	0	0	42		504
0	0	0	0	0	42		504
92	0	250	20	32	548		6,580
,104	0	3,000	240	384	6,580		

PERSONAL INCOME & LIVING EXPENSES

JACK & MARY	November 2012	PREPARED BY: TOMMY MURPHY, ADVANCED CORPORATE TRANSFORMATIONS

NUMBER IN HOUSEHOLD		ADULTS	2		CHILDREN	2

				Monthly	Annual
	Household (all earners) Salary Income			€	€
1	Net Salary Income	Jack		3,717	44,604
2	Net Salary Income	Mary		800	9,600
3	Childrens Allowance			280	3,360
				4,797	**57,564**
	Household Costs (excl. Mortgage)				
1	*Insurance/Pensions*				
	-	Mortgage protection / life cover		125	1,500
	-	House Insurance		185	2,220
	-	Life Insurance		440	5,280
	-	PHI Insurance (Critical Illness & Income Protection)		0	0
	-	Pension 1		0	0
	-	Pension 2		0	0
2	*Children Costs*				
	-	Childcare		40	480
	-	Education		100	1,200
	-	Clothing / Footwear		70	840
	-	Medical		25	300
	-	Other		30	360
3	*Light and Heat*				
	-	Electricity		172	2,064
	-	Gas / Oil		385	4,620
4	*Phone Costs*				
	-	Land Line		110	1,320
	-	Mobile 1		40	480
	-	Mobile 2		20	240
	-	Broadband / Internet		40	480
5	*TV Costs*				
		TV Licence		12	144
		TV Channels		35	420
6	*Household*				
		Food / Shopping Costs		766	9,192
		Housekeeping (if applicable)		200	2,400
		Waste Charges		65	780
		Laundry / Drycleaning		25	300
		Clothing / Footwear (Adults)		200	2,400
7	*Healthcare*				
	-	Health Insurance Costs		300	3,600
	-	Medical (Adults)		75	900
8	*Car Costs*				
	-	Car 1 Petrol / Diesel		85	1,020
	-	Car 1 Insurance		0	0
	-	Car 1 Tax		0	0
	-	Car 1 Repairs, Maintenance		0	0
	-	Car 1 Loan Repayments		0	0
	-	Car 2 Petrol / Diesel		80	960
	-	Car 2 Insurance		50	600
	-	Car 2 Tax		28	336
	-	Car 2 Repairs, Maintenance		0	0
	-	Car 2 Loan Repayments		0	0
9	*Other Loans*				
	-	Personal		0	0
	-	Credit Card		0	0
	-	Savings		0	0
	-	Charitable Donations		0	0
	-	Other		0	0
10	*Other*				
	-	Repairs & Maintenance		165	1,980
	-	Social / Entertainment		150	1,800
	-	Club membership - GAA / Golf		0	0
	-	Household Charge		8	96
	-	Other		0	0
				4,026	**48,312**
			NET	**771**	**9,252**

Acknowledgements

From the bottom of my heart I want to thank all of the people who, having read *Shepherd's Pie*, took the time to contact me. It was your stories, your individual struggles that inspired me and motivated me to share more of my story and experience on a practical level, so that it might make a real difference to someone. Your decision to write to me, email or call me triggered this book.

Sincere thanks also to Seán Dunne and Tommy Murphy from Advanced Corporate Transformations Limited for helping me to rediscover my love of business. Thank you for the priceless education I have received. I can't stress enough the impact that you guys have had on helping me shape my own future, both in my business and personal life.

A number of people in the banking sector as well as private business have been helpful and generous with their time with me over the last eighteen months. Your assistance and forward thinking is very much appreciated.

A massive thanks to Clodagh Feehan, my editor, my advisor on this book, my human spell checker, my filter and controller of my ego. Fancy the trilogy? Thanks also to all at Mercier Press for understanding that my story was not yet finished. Small really is beautiful.

To all my new and existing customers, who demonstrated such goodwill by purchasing their car from the Mordaunt Group after our story went public – you helped us to recover. Thanks also to Amanda Doyle and Ciarán Hayes. I really do appreciate the job you are doing, often in difficult circumstances.

Sarah, I thank you again for everything. Eleven years working together now. Well done.

As always, huge thanks to all my family, especially my parents and my brother Brian, for allowing me to continue telling this story. You are as brave and supportive as ever and I am eternally grateful.

To Emily and George, my beautiful kids. You started this recovery. I love you both so very much.

Anne. Hand in hand. Shoulder to shoulder – forever. I love you. I hope you like your chapter! Thank you from the bottom of my heart once again, for allowing me to share so much of our life story.

Finally to the people of Ireland, whoever, wherever. Believe that recovery is possible and don't give up. There is a way forward. This story is proof. Ireland will prevail and so can you. Create your recovery and own it.